# CRYPTOCURI
# INVESTING IN THE TIME OF
# AUTONOMY

## An Easy Cryptocurrency for Dummies Guide to Wealth Generation the Next Digital Era

By

**GEORGE STALLION**

The trademarks that are used are without any consent, and the publication of the trademark is without permission or backing by the trademark owner. All trademarks and brands within this book are for clarifying purposes only and are owned by the owners themselves, not affiliated with this document.

# TABLE OF CONTENTS

# Introduction

As Cryptocurrencies gain popularity, an increasing number of people are exploring these emerging technologies. The cryptocurrency space is complex, exciting, and brimming with opportunity. However, it can also be very perplexing for beginners.

Most of the knowledge available about cryptocurrencies presupposes any familiarity with cryptography, financial markets, computer programming, and mathematics in general. This book takes a unique approach. Rather than remaining theoretical, we will concentrate on the practical: What exactly is Bitcoin? How can we use it? Why would we wish to do so?

Cryptocurrency is also not mainstream due to its complexity of use. I came across an example of this a few days ago. I needed to migrate some USDC through a network other than the one I normally use. It did not appear in my account, so I looked into it. I discovered and corrected the cause, only to discover that a previous move had been stalled there as well. The last payment was 1.509 Eth, which was worth about $300 at the transaction time. When I discovered the Eth, which I had forgotten I had, it had increased in value to $3,600.

I cashed in about $60k in crypto assets just over a year ago to purchase a home in Spain. Apart from a few weeks, I have spent very little time in it due to the Covid. I can live with that, but the infuriating part is that those crypto assets would have been worth about $300,000 today had I not cashed them in.

I have been trading for over 20 years, and in my 20 years of investing, nothing has caught my eye more than the emerging cryptocurrency technology. I put all my efforts and resources into understanding how these digital currencies and cryptocurrency mechanisms work and how one can benefit from these emerging currencies in today's financial world. As of today, I have been involved in the crypto business for the best part of a decade. Being involved in crypto research has put me in a position of authority and experience to teach the people interested in this new technology.

This book will not provide you with a wide-ranging understanding of public-key cryptography or hashing algorithms. Rather than that, you will have a firm grasp of the practical use of Bitcoin and the technology that powers it. We will cover the fundamentals of Bitcoin and other cryptocurrencies, like what it is, how it functions, why people use it, and how to use it. Additionally, we will look at how to earn money using Bitcoin, other cryptocurrencies, and the emerging markets in this space.

On the one hand, Bitcoin is a difficult concept to grasp. Under the hood, some pretty bizarre math occurs. However, on the other hand, Bitcoin is extremely easy to use! You do not have to grasp any aspect of how a car functions to drive. Likewise, you do not have to be a computer genius to purchase, sell, or invest in Bitcoin.

At the time of writing this book, there were more than 2,000 cryptocurrencies. Cryptocurrencies received widespread media attention in 2017 when Bitcoin's value increased by 1,318 percent. This boom pales compared to the gains made by some other digital properties, such as Ripple, which increased by a whopping 36,018 percent (hold your breath). These returns double what a typical stock investor would earn in a lifetime, and they sparked enough excitement to spark true hysteria.

However, the bubble exploded at the start of 2018, leaving several late buyers out of pocket after purchasing cryptocurrencies at an exorbitant price. That was sufficient for some newbie investors to call the entire industry fraud and abandon investing altogether or return to more conventional financial assets such as stocks. Regardless, the cryptocurrency industry continued to evolve and stabilize, garnering the interest and sponsorship of numerous major financial institutions worldwide and in the United States. If more people gain access to cryptocurrencies, more merchants will feel comfortable accepting them as payment, which will help the entire industry thrive.

**Is now an appropriate time to invest in Bitcoin and other cryptocurrencies?**

That question was posed to me the other week. To comprehend the answer, we must first comprehend the cryptocurrency market. Over the last decade, the cryptocurrency industry has seen spectacular leaps before settling into a range in anticipation of the next major leap.

We are now in a time of recovery after a massive leap. I am not sure if we are at the bottom of the settling time yet, but we are certainly far off the top.

If you were looking to invest regularly, I would tell you to go ahead. However, if you want to invest a single lump sum, it might be prudent to wait a few weeks to ensure the market has settled. Of course, this will undoubtedly have changed by the time you read this book.

Blockchain technology serves as the framework for cryptocurrencies such as Bitcoin; it is the infrastructure upon which cryptocurrencies are founded. Blockchain is a game-changing technology that many say is more important than the Internet's inception. However, blockchain applications do not end with cryptocurrencies, just like the Internet's applications do not end with text.

What makes cryptocurrency investment and trading special is that crypto is a hybrid of an asset (such as stocks) and a currency (like the U.S. dollar.) Thus, analyzing the fundamentals of a cryptocurrency is quite unlike analyzing the fundamentals of every other financial asset. The conventional methods of valuing assets do not operate in the crypto industry, mostly because the crypto data is often not processed in a centralized location. Indeed, most cryptocurrencies and the underlying blockchain technology are decentralized, which means no central authority controls them. Rather than that, power is distributed among the participants in a particular blockchain or crypto group.

The content of this book precludes technical information to facilitate comprehension for those unfamiliar with this technology. Certain words include a professional background in information technology, but they are also well explained. This book uses simple language to prevent misunderstanding, and it will take you by the hand and show you, step by step, how digital currency was born.

To facilitate the comprehension, we will review the past of finance and then discuss what precipitated the birth of many cryptocurrencies in today's society. Following that, we will examine the theory and motivations of the Bitcoin creator. Then, in greater detail, the potential of crypto trading will be examined. Following that, we will walk you through the crypto family and different cryptocurrencies available in the market. After this, an introduction to the Blockchain and the purpose it serves will be discussed. Finally, we will explain what future does cryptocurrency holds and how you can profit through it.

In the final chapters, we will delve further into Blockchain and learn how to conduct business. Following that, we will examine why this technology will change the world by examining business applications and potential banking systems. Finally, a brief explanation will make you familiar with the potential future of Bitcoin, Blockchain, and Cryptocurrency. So, let us explore this exciting world of Cryptocurrency.

# Chapter 1: The History of Finance – B.C. – Before Crypto

Have you ever heard about the term Crypto Currency or Bitcoin before? It is quite a popular word in today's time. I always had a keen interest in money and liked to find out how it worked. This created a keen sense of interest in the financial markets in my head. I used to buy different financial magazines during my school years to learn more about the currencies and mechanisms of money. However, I have come a long way from trading the stock market and am currently investing in cryptocurrencies and the stock market. Learning about Cryptocurrencies took many years of effort and research. I faced many hurdles and failures, but my curiosity made sure I kept pursuing my goals. However, very special credit goes to a friend, John, who helped me establish the basic information on the crypto market.

John lives an easy lifestyle in the south of France. He is a well-learned and successful investor in cryptocurrencies, as he was in almost from the start. The last few years have been incredibly profitable for him. His Bitcoin value increased almost tenfold in the last year alone.

John saw some incredible gains in the value of his Bitcoin. Bitcoin is the major type of Cryptocurrency. John invests in many different cryptocurrencies, i.e., Bitcoin, Monero, Ethereum, Tezos, Iota, and Cardano. However, he has made the most gain on Bitcoin. John explained to me that Cryptocurrency, or Bitcoin for that matter, is not an actual currency. It is a digital form of currency. Digital currency means that cryptocurrency allows you to make online forms of payment produced by numerous people globally. Your cryptocurrency will allow you to make peer-to-peer transactions in a matter of seconds. These digital payments can be made worldwide for free or for very little cost.

John taught me that cryptocurrency is not supported by any physical or tangible asset like gold or silver – crypto is an asset in itself. Furthermore, Bitcoin is an open-source asset. Open-source asset means that any user of Bitcoin can access it. John started his Bitcoin experience in a simple way. He created an e-mail address, got a good internet connection, and used some money. However, cryptocurrency and bitcoin have their highs and lows. Therefore, care must be taken while entering the crypto market.

Do you know anyone investing in cryptocurrency like John? Are you curious about this new technology? Is it something which at the back of your mind, there is a little niggle telling you this is something you will need in the future?

Have you ever been curious about the nature of Money or why it exists? To understand cryptocurrencies, we will need to start from scratch. So let us look at a more basic concept first.

Money is the primary medium of exchange for the exchange of value or something of value.

Anything that serves as a medium of trade is referred to as Money. Anything that can be widely accepted as a means of payment qualifies as a medium of trade.

Long before money was invented, people were happy to create, do, and develop things for one another. They may practically remember what was exchanged in isolated places in terms of receipts and payments. Keeping track of and tallying these transactions aided in meeting the primary requirement of determining who had been billed and who owed Money.

However, as populations grew, so did the number of exchanges. Additionally, when people created items for the common good and rulers began levying taxes, accounting became more difficult to monitor.

Improved techniques, such as the use of metal components as financial instruments, were eventually discovered. The price of rare metals was higher than the price of common metals. Gold and silver, which do not rust, topped the list. Then countries started minting their currencies (varying-weight metal coins bearing their official seal). Although the metal coins and parts were more convenient to store and transport than the previous process, they were also more susceptible to theft.

Governments gradually introduced "fiat currency" as legal tender, as gold and silver were no longer covered. It was entirely based on confidence, in the sense that civilians were compelled to do so. Fiat money has no intrinsic value and is solely a product of the state. All of the Money we currently possess is in the form of fiat currency

In the 1990s, the Internet was gaining popularity, and financial processes were becoming more digitalized. Since there was still some fear surrounding fiat currencies, which were perishable and susceptible to theft, banks advised people to go digital. Additionally, it was not anticipated that paper notes would be printed during this period. Money became digital numbers in banks' computer networks. Today, banks will be in serious trouble if all account holders went to their bank and demanded currency notes equal to the balance of money in their accounts. Compared to the amount of digital currency in circulation worldwide, the total amount of physical Money is extremely small. The world is now moving to a relatively new and more sophisticated form of money known as Crypto-currency. It has gained tremendous popularity globally, and many businesses have started accepting crypto as a form of payment. As per the latest information, Venezuela has dropped the Bolivar and its ties to the U.S. dollar and linked its national currency to Bitcoin.

# 1.1 A Brief History of Crypto

Bitcoin was the first Cryptocurrency ever created! You have probably heard about Bitcoin more than any other cryptocurrency. Bitcoin was the initial result of the first blockchain created by an anonymous person known as Satoshi Nakamoto. In 2008, Satoshi Nakamoto proposed the concept of Bitcoin, describing it as a "purely peer-to-peer version" of electronic currency.

While Bitcoin was the first Cryptocurrency to be created, numerous attempts to create digital currencies existed years before Bitcoin was formally implemented.

Bitcoin and other cryptocurrencies are generated through a process called mining. In stark contrast to mining ore, mining cryptocurrencies requires powerful computers to solve complex problems.

Until 2011, Bitcoin was the only Cryptocurrency. Then, when Bitcoin enthusiasts began to see vulnerabilities, they decided to create alternative coins, also known as altcoins, to improve the design of Bitcoin in the areas such as speed, stability, and anonymity. Litecoin was one of the first altcoins, aiming to be the silver to Bitcoin's gold. However, over 1,600 cryptocurrencies are available at the time of writing, and the number is expected to grow in the future.

Did you know that the world's first cryptocurrency transaction took place on May 22, 2010? On that day, a developer named Laszlo Hanyecz purchased two Papa John's delivered pizzas for 10,000 Bitcoin (BTC). Interesting, no? That amount of Bitcoin would be worth more than half a billion dollars today!

You will learn more about digital currencies in the coming chapters. Now, let us take a step back and dive into the history of money.

## 1.2 Defining Money

Before delving into the details of cryptocurrencies, it is necessary to understand the concept of currency. Money's philosophy is similar to the "what came first: the chicken or the egg?" debate. Money must possess a variety of characteristics to be valuable, including the following:

- It must be available to a sufficient proportion of the population.
- It must be accepted as a form of payment by merchants.
- Society must have confidence that it is important and will remain valuable in the future.

Of course, when you traded your chicken for shoes in the past, the exchanged products had intrinsic values. However, the introduction of coins, cash, and credit cards altered the concept of money and, more significantly, the confidence model for money.

Now that cryptocurrencies exist, the traditional, government-backed currency, such as the U.S. dollar, must be referred to as fiat currency. Fiat currency is described as legal tender such as coins and banknotes that have value solely because the government declares them to have value.

Money is something that is used as a medium of exchange. For example, tennis balls would have been Money if most people and businesses began accepting them as payment.

**Money serves three key functions.** First, by definition, it is a trade channel and a medium of exchange. Additionally, it serves as a currency unit of measure and a store of value.

### A Medium of Transaction`

The exchange of products and services in markets is one of humanity's most fundamental practices.

To reinforce these transactions, people choose something to act as a medium of exchange — they choose something to act as Money.

We can understand the medium of exchange by the example of Cigarettes used as currency in Jails. In most of the jails in the U.S., if one person wanted to get food or medicine or if he had to use a phone in the jail illegally, he had to pay the currency of jail to his inmates, the inmates would accept cigarettes as a medium of exchange to provide goods or services.

When we consider the absence of a medium of exchange, we may appreciate its importance. When goods are exchanged solely for other goods, this is referred to as barter. Since no single item serves as a medium of exchange in a barter economy, prospective buyers must locate items that specific sellers will approve. For example, a purchaser could locate a seller willing to exchange two turkeys for a pair of shoes. Another vendor may be willing to provide you with a hairstyle in exchange for a water hose. Consider for a moment how difficult it would be to live in a barter economy, and you can understand why human societies eventually preferred anything more than one thing — a medium of trade.

## A Currency Unit of Measure

Money serves the purpose of a unit of value, a structured system for determining the worth of items. When someone in the United States is asked how much they have paid for something, they will respond with a dollar amount: "I paid $75 for this device," or "I paid $15 for this pizza." No one will ever say, "I have paid five cups of flour for this phone." Although that assertion is logically correct in terms of the opportunity cost of the transaction, we do not report prices in that manner for two primary reasons. One is that individuals do not walk into a store holding five cups of flour hoping to purchase a phone. The other explanation is that the information acquired would be rendered useless. Others do not comprehend what we meant because they do not see values through flour as a currency. Rather than that, we quantify the worth of things in monetary terms.

## A Store of Value

Money's third characteristic is that it acts as a store of value or an asset that holds its value over time. An example would be when I found a $100 bill in the pocket of my jeans that I wore a few years back, I was overjoyed. The reason for my joy was the fact that the bill was still valuable. That small piece of paper had, in fact, "stored" value.

Money, as a store of value, may serve as a basis for future payments. For example, when you make loans, you typically enter into a deal agreeing to repay the debt in installments. Since Money serves as a store of value, these transfers will be made with Money.

# 1.3 Barter Trading

Bartering is a term that refers to a simple trade, such as exchanging wool for milk. In ancient times, direct trade was an economically viable structure. The disadvantages of bartering became evident as communities progressed. If you traded directly, you could obtain milk only when another cow owner needed wool and vice versa.

The first forms of Money, IOUs (etymology: "I owe you"), were fashioned from stones, feathers, and animal teeth. This allowed members of the same community to exchange goods and services using an intermediary object that could be reclaimed by the subsequent person, just like we do today with Money.

Barter was done by exchanging wheat for medicine or oranges for wheat. This trade was only successful if both the parties' interests were the same and wanted to give and take the same things.

Assume that you live in a barter economy and go grocery shopping. You would need to load a truck with items that the store would consider in exchange for grocery shopping. That would be an extremely challenging proposition. You would have no idea which items the merchant would agree to exchange before you arrived at the store. Indeed, in a barter economy, the complexity and the cost of visiting a store will almost certainly be prohibitively high.

As long as one had the products the other wanted and was willing to accept the item the second person was offering, it was fine and dandy, but what if someone allergic to wheat needs medicine that the other person does not have? Consider the following scenario: Rachel is aware that Alice has wheat and requires medicine, but Rachel is also aware that she has grapes but does not have medicine.

The exchange does not function in this instance. As a result, they must track down a third person, Monica, who may need grapes and may also have excess medicine.

It was never easy to find someone who could move smoothly into the puzzle, as Monica did in the previous example. Nevertheless, this obstacle had to be overcome. As a result, individuals came to embrace a commoditized system of value exchange. Everyone would need a few basic items, such as milk, salt, seeds, and sheep. This system was nearly flawless. However, individuals soon found that storing such products was inconvenient and difficult.

Money had to be standardized. It had to be represented by something divisible, compact, and long-lasting. As a result, the gold standard was established.

## 1.4 Shifting Towards Fiat Currency

The gold standard was a financial system in which the value of a nation's currency was inextricably linked to the value of gold. Under the gold standard, countries agreed to trade paper money for a fixed amount of gold. A gold-standard nation establishes a fixed gold price and purchases and exchanges gold at that price. The fixed price establishes the currency's value. For example, if the United States establishes a price for gold of $500 an ounce, the currency is worth 1/500th of an ounce of gold.

No nation now uses the gold standard on an official basis. For example, the U.K. stopped using the gold standard in 1931, and the United States did the same in 1933 before fully abandoning the system in 1973.

Fiat Money is government-printed Money not backed by a tangible commodity like silver or gold but by the issuing state. A fiat economy is a financial system in which the currency's value is not tied to any tangible asset but can fluctuate dramatically concerning other financial instruments traded on the foreign exchange markets.

Let us examine Daniel's case to have a better idea about fiat currency. Daniel has a particular interest in storing different valuables. However, he regards all his valuables as "Fiat Money." These valuables include the following items:

- Some gold bricks were gifted to Daniel on his 25th birthday by his father. Daniel is now 80 years old.

- An antique painting that was gifted to Daniel by his friend 30 years ago.

- Daniel also has a habit of collecting rare antique coins. He has been collecting these coins for a very long time now. These coins are from different nations, including Greece, Britain, and the States. Unfortunately, some of the coins are so old that they are close to being rusted away.

- Apart from his native currency, i.e., pound sterling, Daniel also keeps some $100 bills in his wallet. He can get these dollars exchanged with his native currency anytime he wants.

According to the above scenario, Daniel has four different types of valuables at present: Gold, antique painting, ancient coins, and the present paper money. Do you think he is right to regard all four categories as fiat money?

If your answer is no, then which of the above valuables do you think should be regarded as fiat money? Of course, only the sterling pounds and the $100 notes are fiat money. The rest can be treated as commodities. But why is that so?

The value of Fiat Money is determined by the association between demand and supply and the sustainability of the issuing country, not the value of the underlying commodity, as is the case for commodity money. Accordingly, most international paper currencies, pounds, and other major world currencies are Fiat currencies.

- State-issued Fiat money is not backed by anything tangible, such as gold.

- Since central banks can dictate how much money is printed with Fiat money, they influence the economy.

- Most paper currencies, including the U.S. dollar, are Fiat currencies.

- One risk of fiat money is that policymakers print too much, leading to hyperinflation.

In Daniel's scenario, gold bricks, antique paintings, and the rare ancient coins are not fiat money because they are tangible assets. The government does not support them in terms of their value, and they are not controlled by the demand and supply forces.

Fiat money has value only if, on its value, the government retains it or two parties to a contract settlement. Governments used to make coins from valuable physical assets, such as silver or gold, or print banknotes that could be exchanged for a fixed amount of usable physical commodity. Fiat money is non-transferable, unredeemable.

Because Fiat money is not bound to physical reserves such as a national silver or gold inventory, it is vulnerable to inflation and becomes worthless in hyperinflation.

When people lose trust in a currency, the currency loses its value. This contrasts with gold-backed Money, which has inherent value due to the use of gold in jewelry and decoration and the development of mobile gadgets, servers, and aviation equipment.

The U.S. dollar is both Fiat and Legal currency and is authorized for both individual and state currency.

Since Fiat money is not a gold-like finite or fixed resource, central banks have far more control over their output, allowing them to manipulate economic variables such as money velocity, credit supply, interest rates, and liquidity. Thus, for example, U.S. Federal Reserve has a dual mandate to manage inflation and unemployment.

Due to the limited gold supply, a gold-backed currency is generally more resilient than Fiat money.

Every nation today has Fiat money as a legal tender. However, while gold and gold coins may be purchased and sold, they are rarely traded or used for ordinary transactions and are more of a speculative asset.

# Chapter 2: The Dawn of Crypto

After getting an insight into the history and evolution of money in the first chapter, we should now compare them to understand better Satoshi Nakamoto's motivation for creating Bitcoin, a cryptocurrency. Finally, we will expand on Satoshi's claims in the Bitcoin paper in this chapter and elsewhere in the text.

As a Crypto Trader and Instructor, I understand the concerns of readers who want to learn about Crypto but are not too keen to get into the trading part directly. As a teacher and the author of this book, I have taken a unique approach to define Crypto to my readers so they do not have to face the issues they have been facing with other learning platforms. This chapter will start with the discussion on Crypto, and then we will take a step back and discuss the basics of Digital Currency and its mechanism.

For many years, I learned the mechanisms and strategies of the stock market. While trading in stocks, I began developing a particular interest in cryptocurrencies. That was an era when Bitcoin was still a curiosity. So many stock traders whom I had known then were switching to the crypto market. That was when I met John during my visit to France.

John was among the expert crypto traders of his time. However, ever since the beginning, his preference among all cryptocurrencies has been in Bitcoin. Therefore, I started from the basics of Bitcoin and then slowly moved on to the more advanced stuff. Bitcoin was not an overnight success for me. I have had my fair share of failures too.

Nevertheless, persistence and sheer determination paid off eventually. Today I hold a number of my favorite crypto projects.

My ultimate goal is to show you get started in the cryptocurrency market without making the mistakes I made in the early days. As I mentioned in the previous chapter of this book, cryptocurrencies, particularly Bitcoin, have highs and lows. The best way to deal with them is to equip yourself with in-depth wisdom about the matter.

We learned about temples, then governments and banks, and their role in the evolution of barter systems into currency systems. The situation is much the same today. When you take a closer look at these systems, you will notice that the "faith" aspect is the single most important factor that keeps them stable. First, people had faith in temples, then in governments and banks. To process payments, the Internet's entire commerce depends on centralized, trusted third parties today. Even though the Internet was built to be peer-to-peer, people continue to create centralized systems to mirror old practices. Technically, creating a peer-to-peer system in the early 2000s was difficult due to technological maturity at the time. As a result, the cost of transactions, the time it took for a transaction to settle, and other problems associated with centralization became apparent. Transactions meant settlement, which was not the case with physical currencies.

Is it possible to create a digital currency backed by computing resources, similar to how gold-backed the money in circulation? Thanks to Satoshi's Bitcoin, the answer is "Yes." Bitcoin is designed to allow electronic transfers between two parties based on cryptographic evidence rather than confidence based on third-party intermediaries. Because of technical advances, it is now feasible. This chapter will examine how Satoshi Nakamoto designed the Bitcoin framework in 2008 using cryptography, game theory, and computer science engineering principles. The system has been very stable and robust enough to withstand any cyber-attack since it went live in 2009. It has withstood the test of time and established itself as a world currency.

Before we move on, let me share a couple of interesting facts with you. First, did you know that the total and maximum number of Bitcoin is limited to 21 million? Out of this figure, many Bitcoins have been lost with time. In 2013, a British person accidentally threw away his hard drive having over 75000 BTC. It took over four years to mine that 75000 Bitcoin, and their value today would be more than $3.75 billion!

## 2.1 What is Bitcoin?

Just as we can interact with physical currency without the involvement of banks or other centralized institutions, Bitcoin is designed to enable peer-to-peer monetary transactions without trusted intermediaries. You will learn what it is and then how it works later in the chapter.

Let us look at James' example to understand what a typical bitcoin could do for you. James is a close acquaintance of John. James is 40 years old and lives in the USA. Recently, he has switched his mode of payment to digital currency. According to James, he makes all the significant transactions through Bitcoin. For example, recently, he purchased a sports car with his Bitcoin. James stores his Bitcoin in a specialized Bitcoin wallet, and the money is transferred using only blockchain technology. We will talk about the Blockchain later in this chapter, but let us first see how the Bitcoin transactions have benefited James.

- Bitcoin transactions are discreet. This means that James's identity is not revealed with a Bitcoin transaction, unlike traditional payment methods.

- James has greater autonomy using Bitcoin, as he does not have to deal with banks or the government. He can control how he spends his digital money.

- In addition, James can send payment to anyone on a network worldwide without any external authority's approval. This means Bitcoin provides James with a peer-to-peer transaction system.

- He can make payments with a single click on his mobile phone. In short, James only requires internet access to make payments on his Bitcoin.

- James has avoided banking fees such as overdraft charges and account maintenance fees by utilizing Bitcoin for payments.

After looking at James' case, are you beginning to understand the application of Bitcoin? Do you think there would be any other benefits of Bitcoin?

Bitcoin is a decentralized cryptocurrency that is not currency-specific and operates on a global scale. It is fully decentralized in every way — technical, logical, and political. New Bitcoin is mined as transactions are authenticated, and as already discussed above, a maximum of 21 million Bitcoin will ever be generated. To hit 21 million Bitcoin, it will take approximately until the year 2140. Anyone with sufficient computing power can participate in mining and contribute to the creation of new Bitcoin. After the total number of Bitcoin is generated, no new coins can be minted; only those already in circulation can be used. Take note that Bitcoin, unlike national fiat currencies, does not have defined denominations. Bitcoin, by default, can have any value with a precision of eight decimal places. Thus, the smallest unit of Bitcoin is 0.00000001 BTC, abbreviated as 1 Satoshi.

Have you ever considered investing in Bitcoin but backed away from that choice due to a limited budget? Then you might need to reconsider your decision.

We will look at Eva's scenario to understand Satoshi's concept in a better way. Eva lives in the U.K. and has been curious about Bitcoin for some time now.

Once she learned the basics of Bitcoin, she downloaded a wallet to her smartphone and bought some crypto. Eva just learned that like the pound can be divided into pence and U.S. dollar into cents, each Bitcoin could also be divided into the smallest unit known as Satoshi. Each Bitcoin comprises 100 million Satoshis.

Eva also knows that she can purchase Satoshi just as she can get Bitcoin, i.e., through Crypto or online exchanges. She can also use Satoshi cranes, which may provide another way to own cryptocurrency. Eva can keep her Satoshi coins in her Bitcoin wallet in the future.

After some months of learning about Bitcoin, Eva noticed that her 'normal money' did not keep up with Bitcoin's price and could not afford to buy a full Bitcoin. However, much to her delight, Eva was still able to invest in Bitcoin trading. Instead of purchasing the entire Bitcoin that was out of her budget, she purchased it in small fractions. These small fractions are known to be the Satoshis that Eva had already known about during her learning period.

Miners process transactions to create new coins and consume the transaction fee that the party wishing to conduct the transaction is willing to pay. When the total supply of coins exceeds 21 million, miners can verify transactions solely to collect transaction fees. However, suppose anyone attempts to make a transaction without paying a transaction charge. In that case, it will still be mined because the transaction is legitimate (if it is valid at all), and the miner is more interested in the mining incentive that allows him to produce new coins.

Are you curious about how the worth of Bitcoin is determined? When currency was backed by gold, it carried great weight and was easy to value according to gold standards.

When we conclude that Bitcoin is backed by the computational resources used for mining, this is insufficient to explain how it acquires its value. Here is a brief overview of economics necessary to comprehend it.

When fiat currency was first introduced, it was backed by gold. Since people believed in gold, they also believed in currency. After a long period, the currency became fully dependent on governments and no longer backed by gold. Nevertheless, individuals continued to believe in it because they created or contributed to the creation of their democracy. Since governments guarantee its value and the public trusts it, it achieves that value. In an international context, the value of a country's currency is determined by various variables, the most critical of which is "supply and demand." Bear in mind that some countries that printed an excessive amount of fiat currency notes went bankrupt; their economies suffered! There must be a balance, and understanding this requires different economics, which is beyond the reach of this book. Therefore, let us return to Bitcoin for the time being.

However, before we talk about the fluctuation in Bitcoin's price against U.S. dollars, let us get acquainted with the basic supply and demand concept. Did you know that a product's price fluctuates mainly due to a change in supply and demand? In the first scenario, we will look at price fluctuation due to the change in demand.

Suppose Clara lives in Geneva, Switzerland. The prices of eco-friendly products in Geneva, such as solar lamps and rechargeable batteries, are stable for the given moment. Suddenly, several environment protection campaigns take place inside Switzerland, after which the Swiss government bans the use of all environmentally harmful products. Now the Swiss economy witnesses a major inclination of the public towards eco-friendly products.

As the demand for eco-friendly products rises, so do their prices. When Clara compares the old and new prices of solar lamps in Geneva, she notices a 13% increase. Hence, the increased demand pushes the prices upwards.

In the second scenario, we will see how a change in the supply of a product can shift its prices up or down. Imagine you are a sportsperson. Your favorite brand's sports kit is part of your regular workout. One day you hear the news of the labor shortage in the sports industry. Due to a labor shortage, your favorite sports brand must cut its supply of sports products, but the demand remains the same. Since the sports products cannot meet the demand, there will be a shortage of sports goods from the given brand. This shortage in the supply of sports products will push their prices up.

A similar supply and demand mechanism applies to Bitcoin. I will give you my example with regards to the supply and demand forces of Bitcoin. During the years when I was trading in stocks, I would frequently hear about Bitcoin. However, since the concept of cryptocurrency was new then, traders or consumers, for that matter, had little awareness about this form of digital currency.

Therefore, when Bitcoin was first released, it lacked an official price or value to place their confidence. If anyone were to sell it for some U.S. dollars (USD), I would never have purchased them in the first place.

When the exchange began, it gradually established a price, and one Bitcoin was not even worth one USD at the time. Bitcoin is a scarce resource because Bitcoin is mined through a competitive and decentralized method called "mining," They are generated at a fixed rate with a maximum limit of 21 million Bitcoin ever created.

Now, reverting to the game of "supply and demand," the value of Bitcoin began to inflate. Slowly, as the whole world came to believe in it, its price skyrocketed from a few USDs to thousands of USDs. Bitcoin adoption is increasing at a rate never seen before among consumers, retailers, start-ups, and large businesses since they are used as currency. Thus, the value of Bitcoin is strongly affected by "confidence," "adoption," and "supply and demand," with the market setting the price.

The question now is why Bitcoin's value is so volatile at the time of writing and fluctuates so much. A straightforward explanation is supply and demand. We have discovered that there can be only a finite number of Bitcoin in circulation, 21 million and that the rate at which they have been produced decreases over time. Because of this, there is always a supply-demand imbalance, resulting in this volatility.

Additionally, Bitcoins are never exchanged in a single location. There are several exchanges located worldwide, and each exchange has its own set of exchange rates. The indexes you see in a trading platform collect and average bitcoin trading rates from several exchanges. Again, since none of these indexes obtain data from the same set of exchanges, they do not correspond.

Some of the leading Bitcoin exchanges in 2021 include:

- Coinbase
- Binance
- Bitcoin IRA
- Prime XBT

Similarly, the liquidity factor, which refers to the total number of Bitcoin flowing through the market at any given moment, impacts the price volatility of Bitcoin.

At the moment, it is unquestionably a high-risk asset, but it may stabilize over time. For example, consider the following factors that can affect the supply and demand for Bitcoin, and therefore their price:

- The public's trust in Bitcoin and their fear of uncertainty
- Press coverage on both positive and negative Bitcoin news
- Some people hold Bitcoin and do not circulate throughout the market, whereas others constantly buy and sell to reduce danger. Therefore, Bitcoin's liquidity ratio fluctuates.
- Acceptance of Bitcoin by the world's largest e-commerce companies
- Particular countries' prohibition of Bitcoin

If you are wondering whether Bitcoin can crash, then certainly, the answer is "Yes." Numerous countries' currency systems have collapsed in many instances. To be sure, there were political and economic causes for them to crash, such as hyperinflation, which is not the case with Bitcoin, which cannot be produced indefinitely, and the total number of Bitcoin is set. However, Bitcoin can fail due to technological or cryptographic issues.

Let us have an example from recent history. Bitcoin's price recently sank by nearly 30% after the Chinese regulators' announcement to ban payment firms and banks from utilizing cryptocurrencies. However, the real selloff started after Elon Musk, Tesla's founder, revealed his failure to accept Bitcoin against car purchases. Interestingly, Bitcoin once again surged by more than 12% in value after the Tesla owner hinted about developing the Dogecoin.

Keeping all our facts and figures straight, it is important to note that Bitcoin has withstood the test of time ever since its inception in 2008, and there is a chance that it will continue to grow significantly larger over time, but this cannot be guaranteed!

But whatever the case may be, an interesting fact about Bitcoin is that it cannot be banned from circulating. Some countries, including Bolivia, Thailand, Vietnam, and Bangladesh, tried to restrict bitcoin usage. However, other countries such as Russia, Japan, Australia, and Venezuela use Bitcoin just as a fiat currency.

Bitcoin's future appears to be both certain and unstoppable. Nobody knows for certain what will happen, but it seems that Bitcoin has penetrated deep enough into the mainstream that it cannot be reversed. Numerous major industries, including airlines, technology firms, government agencies, and the financial sector, have begun to embrace Bitcoin and, even more importantly, the underlying blockchain technology. The growing demand for skilled blockchain programmers across various industries demonstrates that the blockchain age has arrived.

A new generation of entrepreneurs has emerged in the cryptocurrency and blockchain space, creating novel applications based on Bitcoin as a currency and a technology. Only time can say if Bitcoin as a currency will continue to appreciate and continue to rule the cryptocurrency markets or if a disruptive newcomer will dethrone it. Diversifying your cryptocurrency holdings is seen to improve your chances of choosing a winner.

Cryptocurrency diversification is a routine that I have been practicing for a long time now. I can explain the diversification by endorsing the expression: "don't put all your eggs in one basket." Logic says that if you accidentally drop the basket, no more eggs will be left. The same goes for cryptocurrencies. Crypto diversification means investing in multiple crypto projects instead of placing everything in one or two projects. Right now, I have invested in the following different types of cryptocurrencies:

- Bitcoin (BTC)
- Ethereum (ETH)
- Tezos (XTZ)
- Iota (MIOTA)
- Radix (eXRD)
- Namecoin (NMC)

What do I get from diversifying my crypto portfolio? Following are some benefits I get:

- I protect against risks.
- I gain more knowledge on different crypto projects and coins.
- I have more opportunities to achieve better performance.

Therefore, the crux is that although my priority is Bitcoin, it is prudent to invest in others.

Hearing tales of early Bitcoin adopters who made millions can make newcomers to Bitcoin feel as if they are too late. Though it is unknown if Bitcoin would be the "one coin to rule them all," the promise of blockchain technology is only now starting to gain traction in the mainstream, bubbling to the surface of a vast sea of opportunity. Of course, no crystal ball will reveal the exact shape of the future, but one thing is certain: this is just the beginning. Five or ten years from now, individuals who make prudent investments today might very well be considered "early adopters."

## 2.2 Understanding The Bitcoin Mechanism

Patricia just completed her graduation. Alongside her studies, she had been learning about the Bitcoin investment. She is extremely excited to get started with Bitcoin. Patricia knows that to get started, she needs a good internet connection and a smartphone to download the Bitcoin wallet. Although these wallets come in four different forms, mobile, desktop, hardware, and web, she chose the mobile wallet. According to Patricia, she can store her Bitcoin in her mobile wallet, a software program. However, technically, she knows the Bitcoin is not stored anywhere. Once Patricia has a balance in her Bitcoin wallet, she will get a secret number called a private key. The private key will represent the Bitcoin address of her wallet. Patricia says that her bitcoin wallet will let her send or receive the Bitcoin under her ownership.

Did you see how easily Patricia got started with her Bitcoin? To get started with Bitcoin, no technical knowledge is needed. All you need to do is to download a Bitcoin wallet and get started. When you download and install a wallet on your laptop or mobile device, the wallet automatically creates your first Bitcoin address (public key). You will, and should, produce several more.

If you want to maintain anonymity, then it is recommended that you only use the Bitcoin addresses once. Though it works, address reuse is an unintentional consequence of Bitcoin. Reusing addresses can jeopardize privacy and confidentiality. For instance, if you reuse an address and sign a transaction with the same private key, the receiver can easily and accurately verify that the address is yours. If the same address is used for multiple transactions, they can all be monitored, making it much easier to determine who you are. Bear in mind that Bitcoin is not fully anonymous. It is referred to as pseudonymous, and there are methods for tracing the source of transactions that can expose the owners.

You must provide the person transferring Bitcoin to you with your Bitcoin address. This is extremely safe, as the public key is already public. We know that Bitcoin has no concept of a closing balance and that all transactions are registered. Bitcoin wallets can easily measure their spendable balances since they have the private keys to the public keys used to receive transactions. Numerous wallet providers offer a range of Bitcoin wallets. There are numerous types of wallets, each with a different level of security: mobile wallets, desktop wallets, browser-based online wallets, and hardware wallets. When working with Bitcoin, you must exercise extreme caution about wallet protection. Payments made with Bitcoin are final.

You are probably wondering how stable these wallets are. To be honest, various wallet types provide varying degrees of protection, and it all depends on how you plan to use it. Numerous online wallet services have been compromised.

Enabling two-factor authentication wherever possible is often a good idea. If you are a frequent Bitcoin consumer, it might be prudent to hold small amounts in your wallets and the remainder in a secure location.

An offline wallet, also known as a cold wallet, is not linked to the Internet and thus offers the highest degree of protection for savings. Additionally, there should be adequate backup plans in place for your wallet if you lose your computer/mobile device. Bear in mind that if you lose your private key, you will also lose all related funds.

If you have not entered Bitcoin as a miner running a full node, you could simply be a Bitcoin user or trader. You will undoubtedly need an exchange from which you can purchase Bitcoin using U.S. dollars or other currencies that the exchanges recognize. You should always choose to purchase Bitcoin from a reputable and stable exchange. Numerous examples exist of exchanges that security breaches have compromised.

**Security:**

To help envision the cryptocurrency and Blockchain more clearly, consider Fort Knox. Fort Knox is famous for housing the United States' gold bullion depository. Fort Knox contains a boatload of gold. Fort Knox safeguards this gold with armed guards, blast-proof vaults, and several other onsite security measures. If gold has to be transported, we can envision armored vehicles and soldiers armed with machine guns keeping an eye on the process. It would be incredibly difficult for a thief to break into Fort Knox and steal the gold, not just because of the fortified compound but also because gold is a heavy physical object that would be difficult to transport.

Banks (and many other institutions) have traditionally followed a similar model for asset protection, centralizing everything and relying on layers of security.

However, the vast majority of financial information is now stored digitally as data. Of course, we trust banks to provide the cash necessary to back up the numbers in our bank accounts, but for the vast majority of people, those numbers represent a record of value rather than a physical cash sum stashed in a safe.

Rather than physical vaults, our financial assets are mainly represented by financial data stored in the server of the bank's "digital vault." Banks aim to turn these servers into digital Fort Knox, but this centralized paradigm does not translate well to the new world of digital transactions. Whereas breaking into Fort Knox and stealing gold will require a large amount of dynamite, special equipment, escape vehicles, and Ocean's 11-style finesse, hackers can break into bank servers and steal financial information on a fairly regular basis using only computers. As a result, credit card fraud, identity theft, and data breaches are all serious risks that financial institutions face on a near-daily basis.

Banks continue to add layers of protection to their "digital vaults," though hackers continue to breach them. Fort Knox works well for storing physical tons of gold, but it fails miserably when applied to digital data. So let us take a step back and examine the problem. We can begin to wonder if, rather than secure one central server, there is a better model for storing digital information and processing digital transactions. This is where blockchain technology comes into play.

Each block in the Blockchain is connected to the previous block and is publicly recorded through many different nodes located throughout the world. Therefore, rather than hacking into a single central server and stealing or manipulating data, a hacker will have to modify the entire Blockchain simultaneously through most computers that store it worldwide.

Technically, this would take an enormous amount of computational capacity, rendering it effectively impossible to do under current conditions. Due to the lack of centralized data storage, the blockchain framework is by design stable. If anyone attempts to enter a false transaction, such as giving themselves Bitcoin that does not exist, the numerous computers that manage the Blockchain will notice that the math does not add up. If the math does not add up, the transaction is considered invalid and denied and is not added to the blockchain record.

# Chapter 3: The Mechanism

Let us take a step back and understand the basics of Digital Money.

## 3.1 Digital Money

Before moving on with the concept of digital money, let us look at an example. William has various chores for the day. Among these include the following:

- Payment of utility bill. William plans to make payment from his smartphone.

- William must send money to his son, who lives abroad. He has decided to use PayPal for this purpose. According to William, PayPal provides him with a quick and easy way to send money online to his family. All he needs is his son's e-mail address to transfer his payment.

- William is also planning to shop from Amazon's online platform using his credit card.

- Lastly, he has some $500 bills at home that he must deposit in the bank.

Which of the above options do you think fall in the digital money category?

You are right. All the options other than $500 bills to be deposited at the bank are digital money transactions. The payments through PayPal, credit card, or online bills do not include any tangible use of money. Hence, these payments eliminate the need for physically transferring cash.

Digital currency enables previously unthinkable peer-to-peer value transfers. New currencies will emerge as the basic tenets of massive, systemically significant cross-border social and economic networks.

The advent of these new currencies alters the competitive character of currencies, the international monetary system's architecture, and the function of government-issued public money. The term "money homogeneity" refers to a quantitative easing procedure that results in a degree of consistency among various forms of money. In a convertibility arrangement, the issuer of a money commodity enters into a legally enforceable obligation to swap the instrument at a preset rate with another financial intermediary.

A bank is a great example of an agent who is legally obligated to ensure convertibility. Support protects a financial asset's value while allowing the issuer greater freedom. Supporting arrangements such as money pegs and currency bands are ideal examples. Money is classified into two types: account-based currency and token money. Outside money is a claim on something that does not exist; inside money is cash in a bank account.

Here, we will have an instance to understand this concept better. Liam, a good friend of mine, lives in Ireland. He narrated his story when he went to a bank and had a chat with his accountant. That is when the accountant told Liam about inside and outside money. According to the accountant, Liam's bank deposits are the "inside money," whereas the Irish government's national reserves count as "outside money." This is because Liam's bank deposit is a liability inside the private sector, i.e., the deposits lie with the private bank. These deposits will enable private banks to respond to other's needs of mortgages, car loans, and other loans. The Irish government's central bank reserves, on the other hand, are issued by Ireland's central bank, and so its liability exists with the central bank. The outside money does not form liability for anyone "inside" an economy. (This example is based directly on the inside/outside money concept)

The difference between outside and inside money is determined by the method of payment authentication used to validate the payer's identity. The fact that a variety of securities backs the money does not ensure the full convertibility of those assets, as the issuer may alter its mind at any time. The advent of digital digitalization has the potential to open up new avenues for internationalizing current currencies. For example, all required to trade currency on Alipay's network is a password associated with a certain digital "wallet." A currency may internationalize in two ways: as a global cash store or as a reserve tool. Digital networks are particularly effective in expanding commercial opportunities and spreading information across national borders.

The existence of network ecosystems simplifies invoicing in the platform's currency even further. Digitalization may be an effective approach to internationalizing such currencies as a medium of trade. A country with vast digital networks may uncover new ways for international recognition of its currency. Official currencies will eventually permeate the economy of other countries if a robust digital network supports them. Small economies are vulnerable to dollarization, both traditional and digital, due to a stable currency.

While working with my friend John, he gave me an incredible example of digital currency internationalization. John's friend worked in the USA while his family lived in China. Therefore, his friend opened an account with Alipay's digital wallet and got his U.S. dollars exchanged against the Chinese currency to be sent to his family back home in China. Alipay's account uses SWIFT code, also known as BIC (Bank Identifier Code). The SWIFT ensures that your money is being transferred to the right country, bank, and branch where your account is registered.

# 3.2 Cryptography

Millions around the world today are taking a keen interest in cryptography. Cryptography prevents you from theft, crime and provides your human right to privacy. Just imagine an expert hacker gets all the confidential data of an intelligence agency. Do you think a security breach at such a high level is possible? Or do you agree that the intelligence agency must have had some strong arrangements, such as various encryption systems?

Before moving towards cryptography, we will begin with some simple examples.

Just suppose that you utilize digital money for online shopping. Your electronic money will be encoded to protect your transaction information. Likewise, your credit card authorization will provide confidentiality to your transactions.

Have you got any idea about the term "cryptography" after looking at the above two examples?

Cryptography is the process of encrypting networked devices, web applications, and digital data through coding. It is a concept aimed at ensuring the security and confidentiality of vital information in the case of a data breach. While the term is most often associated with the modern digital era, it has been used in government and military operations for decades. For instance, Navajo code talkers used cryptography to transmit sensitive information in their native tongue during World War II.

Apart from hash functions, asymmetric cryptography is a critical component of the Blockchain's base technology. It serves as the foundation for identifying and protecting Blockchain users.

However, cryptography is commonly regarded as a difficult subject to grasp. As a result, this phase focuses on gradually incorporating cryptography to become intuitive and essential for grasping the Blockchain's meaning of security.

## The Origin

People used conventional mail to send messages long before e-mails, facsimiles, telephones, and messaging apps were invented. Like its modern competitors, traditional mail continues to exist and is used by many people. Postal staff now distributes formal letters by placing them in the recipients' mailboxes. Each of these mailboxes doubles as a trapdoor. Although it is simple to insert a letter into the letter slot by design, removing a letter is extremely difficult. Letter removal is intended to be done exclusively by the addressee who owns the key to the mailbox. This concept has existed for a long period, and we all use it when sending an e-mail to an e-mail address, messaging someone in the most recent chat app, or sending money to a bank account. In both cases, the security concept is based on distinguishing two types of information: publicly accessible information that serves as the address for a trapdoor-like package. Private information serves as the key for opening the box and accessing its contents. When it comes to personal data protection, the Blockchain employs the same principle. Therefore, keeping this metaphor in mind will assist you in navigating the cryptography universe.

## The Goal

The objective is to identify owners and property so that only the legitimate owner has access to it.

## The Obstacle

Since the Blockchain is a peer-to-peer framework, it can be used for all. Anyone can establish a connection to the system and contribute computing resources or additional transaction data. However, it is not desirable for all to have access to the property associated with blockchain accounts. Private property's exclusivity is one of its defining characteristics. The account owner who transfers ownership has the exclusive authority to do so. As a result, the Blockchain's task is to protect the accounts' property while maintaining the transparent architecture of the distributed framework.

Did you understand how blockchain technology supports cryptocurrency? John once told me that ever since he started crypto trading, he noticed the following benefits:

- **Transparency:** The Blockchain makes every single transaction apparent and visible. John can make decisions according to observable activity.

- **Security:** John is a happy crypto trader because his crypto wallets are safe. The reason he noticed is that hackers cannot easily invade. How is that even possible? Blockchain transaction data is spread across a network of computers, and that means little to no chances of failure.

- **Decentralization:** Blockchain technology decentralizes various digital assets. So now, the real decision-making power is in John's hands and not with central authorities, which are not the key players in the game.

Can you think of some other ways the Blockchain backs Crypto? Do you think the cryptocurrency would have been able to maintain its transparency without Blockchain? Let us look further into this concept.

## The Concept

The idea is to treat accounts similarly to mailboxes: anybody can transfer property to them, but only the account owner can access the contents. The most distinctive characteristic of a mailbox is that its location is marked, allowing everyone to put something in it but only the owner to open it with a key. The duality of a public mailbox and a privately owned key has a modern equivalent: public-private-key encryption. One uses public keys to identify accounts that are accessible to everyone, while access is restricted to private keys.

The most important element of cryptography is the construction of ciphers. Ciphers are written codes that conceal sensitive information from those who should not see it. A more powerful cipher results in a more stable system. You can refer to the Morse code example under the earlier heading of cryptography for a better understanding.

In the digital era, the criteria defining data storage, processing, and delivery are continuously changing. Although this expansion simplifies and improves our lives, it also increases the possibility of security breaches and compromises. This technological advancement elevates cryptography to a critical concept and an exciting field for students to investigate. Individuals interested in pursuing a career in cryptography must be able to address the question, "What is cryptography?

Cryptography's primary objective is to prevent unauthorized individuals from accessing data. It functions similarly to door locks or bank safes in that it frequently prevents unauthorized access to their contents. Cryptography, like locks and keys in the physical world, encrypts data using keys.

Encryption is the digital equivalent to the physical act of locking a lock. Thus, decryption is the digital equivalent of the physical act of opening a lock.

As a result, when we discuss cryptography to secure data, we use the terms encryption and decryption to refer to the processes of protecting and unprotecting data. The term "ciphertext" refers to data that has been encrypted. To those unfamiliar with cipher code, it appears to be a meaningless set of letters and numbers.

## 3.3 Bitcoin's Ecosystem

Before you can obtain or spend Bitcoin, you must first create a wallet. Bitcoins are stored in a "wallet," which is a Bitcoin address in the digital realm. There are numerous Bitcoin wallets available, and we will discuss some of the most popular and how to create your own. However, before we discuss how to select and build your Bitcoin wallet, let us take a closer look at how Bitcoin wallets to function.

Cryptography is the study of encrypted communication, and the term "cryptocurrency" contains the term crypto. Modern cryptography is highly based on complex mathematical algorithms that computers have deciphered. Individuals often encrypt their e-mails and communications containing sensitive information so that only the intended recipient can decode them. To a third party, encrypted e-mails seem to be complete nonsense because they would be unable to decrypt the contents unless they have the document's specific password or key.

Although the majority of people associate encryption with digital data, cryptography has existed for centuries. Earlier encryption techniques involved using secret codes to transmit messages through hostile territory, often used by militaries.

The "Caesar Cypher," which Julius Caesar is said to have invented to communicate with his generals, is one of the most frequently used examples of Classical cryptography. The Caesar Cypher is a straightforward substitution cipher.

Certain letters in the original message are replaced with letters a certain number lower than the original, resulting in a sort of "name scramble" that can be deciphered only if the change is known and the process reversed.

Of course, Encryption has evolved into a much more complex mathematical procedure. If we are aware of it or not, we all use different forms of encryption regularly, such as an ATM PIN to access your bank account or the more common practice of unlocking your phone with a password. In addition, when sending sensitive information, many people use more advanced systems with several layers of strong encryption.

Let us have more clarity about the concept of "encryption" by looking at everyday life examples. Phil uses a mobile password to secure his mobile data. He also uses a specific website password to protect his website data from being hacked. Further, to protect his bank account information, Phil uses a security PIN. The mobile password, ATM PIN, and password to protect his website are good examples of encryption. Phil takes these measures to protect the confidentiality of his information. So, these processes of encryption help Phil to protect his data's security.

To secure Bitcoin wallets, asymmetric encryption, also known as "public-key cryptography," is used. This can sound familiar if you have ever sent encryption encrypted with PGP. However, if this is not the case, have no fear. While some strange math is occurring in the background, the majority of wallets are simple to use.

All necessary Bitcoin wallets are comprised of two components: a public key and a private key. These two keys are created automatically and usually take lengthy strings of random letters and numbers.

## The Public Key

Before moving to public and private keys concerning bitcoin, let us first understand these concepts through a generic example. We all frequently send and receive e-mails in our work lives. So is the case with Amanda and Oliver, who work in different departments of an organization. Oliver wants to send Amanda an encrypted e-mail. For this purpose, Oliver will take Amanda's public key, which would be visible to everyone. After receiving the encrypted e-mail, Amanda will take her private key to decrypt Oliver's message. Her private key will be known only to Amanda. The hackers would not intrude in this way, as they will not have the private key to decrypt the e-mail. Therefore, only Amanda will be able to decrypt Oliver's e-mail.

When it comes to Bitcoin, the public key is the address for your Bitcoin wallet. This is a unique digital address that is like your "Bitcoin e-mail address." Everyone has access to your public key. Individuals can give you Bitcoin using this address, which is also your public key. When you initiate a transaction, the Blockchain will record your public key address. Bitcoins are either transferred into your wallet from another location or are sent from your wallet to the address (i.e., public key) of another wallet. Your public key is almost certainly associated with your identity, either directly or indirectly, depending on the configuration of your Bitcoin wallet. Unless you take conscious steps to protect your privacy, you should expect your public key address to be associated with your identity.

## The Private Key

If the public key corresponds to your Bitcoin "e-mail address," the private key corresponds to your password. Your private key is exclusive to you and enables you to access the contents of your wallet and send Bitcoins to others.

When you send Bitcoin to another party, the transaction is only true if the recipient's public and private keys match. Your private key informs the machine, "Hey, I'm the legitimate owner of this wallet," while your public key informs the machine, "This other wallet is where the Bitcoins should go."

You must protect your private key. If anyone else obtains access to your private key, such as a hacker, they would be able to exploit your funds. You can do nothing in this case, which is why it is important to keep your private key safe. Unlike an e-mail password, you cannot simply "reset" a lost private key, so exercise caution. If you misplace your private key, there is no chance of recovering it, and you will be unable to use your bitcoin.

# Chapter 4: The Crypto Family

The cryptocurrency sector is infamous for its volatility. Things change on a daily basis, and new currencies are created regularly. What is innovative one day may be regarded as obsolete the next. Having said that, certain digital currencies have demonstrated relative stability. While Bitcoin is commonly regarded as the market leader in blockchain-based currencies, many new currencies have grown in popularity in recent times. These new cryptocurrencies are also referred to as Altcoins.

## 4.1 Altcoins

Remember, in the previous chapter, I told you about cryptocurrency diversification. I also mentioned some advantages associated with diversification. After achieving the milestone of Bitcoin success, I kept compelling myself to think of a way to expand. That is when the idea of diversification came to my mind. After thorough research into the matter, I found that Altcoins would be my next best alternative. My friend John, who was instantly attracted to my idea of diversifying my crypto portfolio, asked me what brought me to Alcoins' decision. I told him that Altcoins would provide me alternative options and bring innovation to my portfolio. Also, I was among some of the very few people at the time to invest in Altcoins. The idea was relatively new, so it gained good attention from people. But they were waiting for some positive feedback before investing.

For your knowledge, I started with Namecoin. Namecoin was the first Altcoin created in April 2011. Just like Bitcoin, you can obtain Altcoins in a variety of ways. I started by creating an exchange account where I got access to my Altcoins. Well-established altcoins, such as XRP and Ether, are good competitors to Bitcoin.

Altcoins are alternative cryptocurrencies to Bitcoin. They share certain traits with Bitcoin but vary in other aspects. For instance, certain altcoins generate blocks or validate transactions using a different consensus process. Alternatively, they differentiate themselves from Bitcoin by introducing new or enhanced features, such as smart contracts or reduced price volatility.

As of March 2021, around 9,000 cryptocurrencies existed. Altcoins accounted for more than 40% of the global cryptocurrency market in March 2021, according to CoinMarketCap. Due to its genealogy in Bitcoin, altcoin price fluctuations tend to mirror Bitcoin's. However, analysts believe that as cryptocurrency investing ecosystems mature and new markets for these coins arise, price movements for altcoins will become independent of Bitcoin's trading signals.

Let us have a scenario here. Mark, a successful trader in Bitcoins, says to his partner trader, "Hey, let us expand our crypto trading," and so, they both decide to invest in altcoins. While figuring out which one to invest in, Mark and his crypto trading partner decide to go with the altcoins that share various common characteristics with Bitcoins. "Of course, this makes it easier for us to understand the alternative cryptocurrency's mechanism in a better and faster way, as we already know about Bitcoins," claims Mark. The Altcoin they have chosen uses a common system of "halving" with the Bitcoin, which reduces the coins in circulation.

Meanwhile, the two partners also notice that their chosen altcoins change their prices with Bitcoins. As the BTC price spikes, so does the price of their altcoins and vice versa. "It is more like the paper money that would depend upon the gold prices in the past era," informs Mark. Which Altcoin do you think Mark and his partner have invested in? It is interesting to note that not all altcoins have their values fixed according to Bitcoins.

The term "Altcoin" is a mashup of the alternatives "alternative" and "coin" and refers to all cryptocurrencies other than Bitcoin. Bitcoin and altcoins operate on a similar fundamental structure. They exchange code and operate as peer-to-peer systems or as a massive computer capable of simultaneously processing vast amounts of data and transactions. In some cases, altcoins strive to be the next Bitcoin by providing a low-cost method of conducting digital transactions.

**However, there are numerous distinctions between the two entities.**

James has been my talented student. He got cryptocurrency training from me for about two years. While entering the cryptocurrency market, I suggested James invest in Bitcoins and altcoins side-by-side. While Bitcoin has been the king of cryptocurrency for a long, altcoins have brought in innovation and unique-use cases. Consequently, Bitcoin has responded by making new improvements and creating a healthier market. And likewise, after entering the crypto market, James found out that although Bitcoin may be the king, it still had shortcomings that the altcoins overcame.

Bitcoin was one of the earliest cryptocurrency implementations, and its philosophy and design set the standard for the development of subsequent cryptocurrencies. However, its implementation suffers from several flaws. For example, Proof-of-Work (PoW), the consensus mechanism used to build blocks, is inefficient in terms of energy and time. Additionally, Bitcoin's smart contract possibilities are restricted.

Altcoins overcome Bitcoin's perceived constraints to gain a competitive edge. For example, numerous alternative altcoins employ the Proof-of-Stake (PoS) consensus method to reduce energy consumption and the time necessary to produce blocks and confirm new transactions.

James happened to visit me about a year after he had joined the crypto market. I asked James about his experience with the altcoins, and he talked about Ether. Earlier, I had told him about Ether to be the world's second-largest cryptocurrency by market capitalization utilized in smart contracts on Ethereum as gas (or payment for transaction expenses). Through his practical experience in the field, James further learned that altcoins address long-standing criticisms about Bitcoin. For example, stable coins lack the price fluctuation associated with Bitcoin, making them excellent for daily transactions.

After listening to my student's above-given views and findings, I told him that altcoins had established a market for themselves by establishing this distinction from Bitcoin. As a result, they have drawn investors who regard them as credible alternatives to Bitcoin. "So, how do the investors gain confidence in altcoins after years of trading in Bitcoins?" Inquired James. "Well, investors are confident because they anticipate profit as altcoins gain popularity and consumers, as well as a price appreciation," I told my student.

When I asked James about his perspective about whether altcoins are worth it, he discussed the highs and lows of these cryptocurrencies with me.

**Pros:**

- According to James' observation about altcoins, they are generally created to remedy a perceived weakness in the Bitcoin architecture, whether it is the efficiency, mining cost, or another element.

- Secondly, he learned that altcoins provide competition. To further test his knowledge, I asked him, "How come?" to which James replied, "By altering the rules that govern Bitcoin, altcoin developers provide room for new rivals in the 'Bitcoin system."

- According to James, "Another plus point of altcoins is the low transaction fees." He elaborated that in addition to the security provided by blockchain technology, one of the advantages of utilizing altcoins as a payment method is the comparatively low transaction fees associated with each transaction.

- "Also, an altcoin may fit into more than one class," said James.

My student then went on with the limitations of altcoins.

**Cons:**

- Altcoins are quite volatile in terms of value: their value might fluctuate significantly as a new investment.

- Altcoins, like Bitcoin, are often the target of frauds and other bogus schemes.

- Altcoins are classified and categorized according to their functions and consensus procedures.

I was glad that my student was learning about the crypto market at a good pace. However, James was an amateur at the time but was a quick learner. Also, the right direction is all that matters, after all.

You might be curious to know which Altcoin is best to invest in. Here's a quick rundown of some of the most significant types of altcoins.

**Mining-Oriented**

As its name implies, mining-based altcoins are typically mined through mining. The majority of mining-based altcoins build blocks using Proof-of-Work, a mechanism in which systems earn new coins by solving difficult challenges.

Litecoin, Monero, and Zcash are all examples of mining-based altcoins. In early 2020, the majority of the leading altcoins were mining-based.

Pre-mined coins are an alternative to mining-based altcoins. These coins are not generated by a methodology but are distributed before being listed on cryptocurrency exchanges. Ripple's XRP is an instance of a pre-mined cryptocurrency.

## Stablecoins

Since the beginning, Cryptocurrency transactions and use have been characterized by volatility. Stablecoins seek to mitigate this general volatility pegged to a basket of products, such as fiat money, valuable gems, or other cryptocurrencies. The basket is meant to serve as a reserve for holders if the cryptocurrency fails or has difficulties. Stablecoins' Price variations are not meant to surpass a restricted range.

Diem, the stablecoin created by social networking juggernaut Facebook, is the most well-known example. It is a coin backed by the U.S. dollar. Other stablecoins are MakerDAO and USDC.


## Utility Tokens

Utility Tokens are those that are utilized to deliver services inside a network. They could perhaps be used to pay for services or redeem prizes, for example. Unlike security tokens, utility tokens do not provide dividends or need a stake in the underlying asset. For example, Filecoin is a form of utility currency. It is used to acquire network storage space.

## Security Tokens

Like securities traded on stock exchanges, Security tokens have a digital origin. Security tokens are similar to traditional equities in that they frequently guarantee investors equity in the shape of ownership or a dividend distribution. The idea of such tokens appreciating at a price is huge money for investors to invest in them. Generally, Security tokens are distributed to investors via initial coin offerings or ICOs.

## 4.2 Ethereum

Earlier, I narrated the success story of my student James. Now let me tell you about another scenario. Sarah, another talented student of mine, also invested in Ethereum. The other day, I met Sarah after a long time. She told me about her activities as a crypto trader. Just like James, Sarah also realized that some types of altcoins had surpassed Bitcoin's features. "Interestingly, Ethereum mining utilizes much lower energy than Bitcoin mining," remarked Sarah. She also referred to a recent blog post from an Ethereum Foundation researcher that stated that the Foundation was working to have Ethereum save up to 99.5 % of the energy it presently consumed.

I agreed with Sarah's statement that Bitcoin is widely considered the leader in blockchain-based currencies, but Ethereum has gained a lot of traction since its inception in late 2013.

If you look at Ethereum's story, Vitalik Buterin, a programmer, created Ethereum. Unlike Bitcoin, which is purely a digital currency, Ethereum is a blockchain-based platform for constructing decentralized apps powered by "smart contracts." So whereas Bitcoin is used as a peer-to-peer electronic payments system, the Ethereum blockchain is used to run the code that powers decentralized applications.

It may help to think of Ethereum from the perspective of a smartphone. Let us suppose you purchase a new smartphone. Your smartphone will come pre-installed with a common operating system, such as iOS or Android. Anyone can design apps that perform a wide variety of functions to operate on that operating system. Ethereum, in this analogy, is comparable to an operating system: it provides a foundation upon which other applications can be built.

One application that runs atop Ethereum is a digital currency called Ether, frequently referred to as "Ethereum." This can be perplexing because both the currency and the platform are commonly referred to as "Ethereum." Still, it is critical to realize that the currency is only one component of the Ethereum blockchain infrastructure. Ethereum "miners" are compensated with Ether for their efforts in maintaining the Ethereum blockchain.

Ethereum mining has operated on a Proof-of-Work consensus methodology similar to Bitcoin since its inception. However, as of 2017, the Ethereum team revealed plans to switch to a Proof-of-Stake mechanism. Understanding the distinction between these two methods of authenticating blockchain transactions is critical for contextualizing some of the most contentious disputes currently raging in the broader blockchain community.

In this part of the book, I have frequently brought up my students who are either successful cryptocurrency traders or are still in the learning process. This is because the concepts I am using in this chapter are frequently asked by my students, especially when deciding which Altcoin one should choose to invest in.

So, before moving on, I would like to introduce another student. Taylor is a student at one of Maryland's state universities. Apart from her academics and university life, she has a keen interest in cryptocurrencies. So, she is also presently taking cryptocurrency training from me. A few days before, Taylor has just learned that in Proof-of-Work, all miners try to solve a complex sum, and the person decides the winner with the most quantity of hardware devices. On the other hand, the Proof-of-Stake randomly selects the winner according to the amount they have staked. Taylor inquired if the Proof-of-Stake model was better than Proof-of-Work.

When we discussed "Proof of Work" as a fundamental part of the Bitcoin protocol, we discussed how Bitcoin miners must invest in specialized mining equipment that consumes a large amount of electricity to solve a block. However, Proof-of-Stake (PoS) operates in a slightly different manner.

A Proof-of-Stake concept is more reminiscent of gambling. Rather than being referred to as "miners," Ethereum is adopting the word "validators." Validators contribute a predetermined amount of their own money (Ether in the case of Ethereum) to the block's solution. The more money validator wagers, the more likely they are to solve the block.

# 4.3 Ripple

We have already discussed how Ethereum differs from Bitcoin in several ways. One point that we have neglected to mention is that, unlike Bitcoin, Ethereum is administered by a central team of well-known individuals. This organization controls what happens with Ethereum, such as the transition from Proof-of-Work to Proof-of-Stake, and hence exerts a greater degree of control over the platform than Bitcoin does. Even so, Ethereum remains an open blockchain platform that anybody can use.

Ripple is another example of a blockchain technology version. Ripple is a two-pronged entity: a cryptocurrency and a blockchain technology firm. Ripple's focus is less on peer-to-peer transactions and more on the financial industry as a whole, collaborating with banks and financial institutions to integrate blockchain technology into their infrastructure.

While Ripple remains fairly divisive among cryptocurrency enthusiasts, it does claim to address some of Bitcoin's shortcomings. Most significantly, Ripple eliminates the verification wait time.

Instant Transactions are possible. However, unlike Bitcoin's "Proof of Work" model, Ripple's consensus model is centralized and relies on a network of "trusted" servers, which raises some serious concerns for individuals interested in blockchain technology to promise decentralized design.

As realized through blockchain technology, the distributed ledger concept represents a fundamental rethink of institutional institutions, moving away from a hierarchical model toward a distributed network. This, according to many investors, is the key to blockchain technology's transformative potential. The ramifications of information decentralization are substantial and probably definitely have not been fully recognized.

## 4.4 Monero

Monero is a cryptocurrency that provides users and their exchanges with a high level of privacy. Monero, like Bitcoin, is a decentralized peer-to-peer cryptocurrency; however, unlike Bitcoin, Monero is considered a more anonymous or privacy-oriented digital cash.

Monero was founded in April 2014 as a fork of Bytecoin without pre-mine or venture capital funding. A fork happens when an original cryptocurrency is divided into two to create a new version, enabled by the open-source formats used in most cryptocurrency designs. The majority of forks are created to address the parent currency's problems and to create superior alternatives.

Monero's popularity has been growing in the cryptocurrency market, mostly due to its anonymity feature. Each cryptocurrency user is assigned a public address or key.

With Bitcoin, the coins are sent to the receiver's address, which the recipient must provide to the sender.

Once the sender has access to the money recipient's public address, he may determine how many Bitcoins the recipient has. In addition, all coins moved from sender to recipient are documented and made public on the Bitcoin blockchain.

However, even if the sender recognizes the recipient's public address, transacting with Monero does not provide the sender with a window into the recipient's holdings. Monero transactions are not traceable or linkable. Coins provided to a recipient are redirected through a randomly generated address created for that transaction alone.

Unlike Monero, the Monero ledger does not store the sender's and recipient's actual stealth addresses. The one-time generated address that is logged in is not linked to either party's actual address. As a result, anyone inspecting Monero's opaque ledger would not determine the addresses and identities of any previous or current transaction.

Monero enables users to choose their level of transparency. Each user has a "view key" that they may use to gain access to their account's private key. A user can provide chosen parties access to his view key with certain restrictions in place, such as access to view the account's holdings but not to spend any cash; access to all past and current transactions; or access to just certain transactions in the account. Parents may require view keys to watch their children's transactions, and the user may grant access to auditors to check his account holdings and value.

Along with the view key, users have a "spend key" that permits the user to spend or transfer monies from the account to a designated entity with whom the user shares the key. Like the view key, the spend key is 64 characters in length and is composed of alphabets and digits.

Monero's popularity has surged, not just among those seeking to engage in criminal activities on the underground market but also among those seeking to purchase goods and services online anonymously. Individuals who do not wish to receive unwanted advertisements based on their purchasing patterns from digital marketers, the rich who hackers regularly target, individuals who purchase sex toys, and sick individuals who want to purchase medications discreetly online are just a few examples of users who might prefer Monero's unique privacy platform over Bitcoin's transparent ledger.

## 4.5 Litecoin

Charlie Lee, a former Google employee, founded Litecoin (LTC) in 2011. Litecoin's software is strikingly similar to bitcoin's, while Litecoin's is quicker. This is one of the reasons for Litecoin's long-term viability.

While mining a bitcoin block takes around ten minutes, mining a Litecoin block takes only two and a half minutes. The supply of Litecoin is set at 84 million, and the current incentive for mining a block is 12 and a half Litecoins — a figure that will halve in 2023.

## 4.6 NEO

NEO, headquartered in China, has an audacious goal of assisting in creating and developing a new digital smart economy.' Its network structure facilitates the development of decentralized applications, or 'Dapps,' that enable various safe and rapid transactions using smart contracts.

Despite the Chinese government's restriction on initial coin offerings and cryptocurrencies, NEO has so far raised the cash necessary to develop and execute its initiatives, fueling conjecture about a possible relationship between the business and the Chinese government.

## 4.7 Stellar

The mission of Stellar, launched in early 2014 by Jed McCaleb and Joyce Kim, is to connect banks, consumers, and payment systems effortlessly, rapidly, and securely. In addition, its platform is meant to enable near-instantaneous money transfers across countries — with its cryptocurrency, XLM, serving as a bridge currency between fiat currencies.

Stripe, one of the world's major payment gateways, revealed intentions to phase out Bitcoin, favoring XLM in early 2018. Stellar's price increased by 20% in response to this announcement, helping to solidify the coin's influence in the market of bitcoin alternatives.

# Chapter 5: Blockchain – Behind the Scenes

Before delving into the technical aspects of Blockchain technology, it is critical to understand the problems that Blockchain addresses. Why do we need Blockchain technology, and what can it do that our present technology cannot?

My friend John once asked me about the need for Blockchain technology. I asked him, "What problems do you face in a traditional baking system?" And after a brief pause, John began,

"Well, if we talk about the cross-border payments, for example, it is a time-consuming process. Also, a hefty sum of money is required if we transfer money across the borders through traditional banking."

I agreed with John, "Yes. As per the World Bank, the average transaction fee for global payments is nearly 7%. And that's a huge amount."

"What else do you think are the limitations of traditional banking?" I asked John.

"There is less transparency. There is more centralization," John assumed.

"If by centralization you mean that governments and central banks are majorly in charge of your data and transactions, and you feel less safe about your privacy, then this is true. It is an issue with the traditional banking systems," I elaborated.

After this dialogue with John, I told him that all these problems end with Blockchain technology. So, in short, to avoid the problems of traditional banking, we get help from Blockchain.

The pioneers of Bitcoin and Blockchain technology recognized a fundamental problem in the way we think about transactions, trust, and social organizations.

The first iterations of Blockchain appeared around the 2007 financial crisis in the United States when many individuals lost faith in social institutions intended to defend the common person's interests.

Of course, people lost faith in the banking system in the aftermath of the crisis. Still, they also lost faith in the government's ability to control financial markets and in the press's ability to probe future catastrophes.

The majority of people would agree that our institutions have problems and do not present ideal solutions. However, they do resolve trust issues and have done so for hundreds of years.

Indeed, we are arguably living in the calmest and comfortable period of human history. Thus, an alternative to our current institutions must demonstrate its advantages and strengths.

Did you know that the first country to issue Blockchain-backed national currency was Tunisia? This happened back in 2015. Senegal and Marshall Islands followed this action in later years. The Swiss city of Zug is known to be the Crypto-Valley. Zug was the world's first city to accept crypto payments for taxation.

The concept behind Blockchain is to replace institutions governed by fallible human beings with technology that is more efficient and empowers individuals as well. If you could design a mechanism for strangers to trust one another without using a bank or a government as a middleman, you would solve one of society's most pernicious blockages. However, to accomplish this, you would need a robust system for establishing consensus between the strangers, as Blockchain developers think that power lies in decentralization.

Essentially, all Blockchain (and other cryptographic technology) applications are built on the principle of decentralization.

- Blockchain tries to redistribute regulatory authority to individuals rather than a rigid, slow central authority making choices and controlling interactions.

- Rather than relying on a single large organization, Blockchain establishes confidence through consensus.

At the beginning of this chapter, I shared with you a dialogue between John and me. We discussed that worldwide payment transfers through traditional banking are costlier. But how much costlier? Did you know that Blockchain transactions are millions of times cheaper than traditional banking transactions? Interestingly, if I transfer 849,999.99939168 Ether, I will pay only $0.19 for the transaction fee. 849,999.99939168 Ether is roughly equal to $1,129,879,499.19. Just imagine, only $0.19 fee for transferring $1,129,879,499.19!

## 5.1 Blockchain – A bubble?

Once, my student, Sarah, told me that the price of bitcoin price spiked greatly after purchasing it. But soon afterward, its value dropped. "Why are the Bitcoin prices so uncertain? Is it a bubble?" When she inquired further, I told her that digital currencies like Bitcoins have virtual existence and have no real value. Their value could be zero, or it could be in millions. No one knows Bitcoin's real value, and this creates uncertainty. Therefore, the uncertainty creates a Bitcoin bubble.

When Blockchain Revolution was published in May 2016, the whole crypto-asset market was worth $9 billion. Ethereum's network value had recently surpassed $1 billion, making it the second blockchain unicorn (after bitcoin).

This was in the early stage. If the crypto-asset market had been a public firm, it would have barely made the S&P 500 index. After less than two years, the crypto asset market had grown to $420 billion in size.

This crypto assets value explosion has caught the interest of developers, entrepreneurs, non-governmental groups, and the media, not to mention governments, central banks, the investing public, and regulators.

Additionally, it has elevated these digital assets (and the underlying blockchain technology), formerly the realm of a few dedicated engineers, to a level of public attention.

Berkshire Hathaway CEO Charlie Munger went so far as to label bitcoin a "noxious poison."

Vitalik Buterin, Ethereum's founder, grabbed the spotlight in late 2017 when the crypto-asset market cap surpassed $500 billion.

**"Have We Earned It?" he tweeted.**

**"How many unbanked folks have we enrolled?"**

**"How much value is kept in smart contracts that do useful tasks?"**

Buterin said, "While activity is increasing, it is not yet big enough to justify the market's size."

**"The answers to all of these questions are most certainly not zero, and in some situations, they are pretty significant," he continued.**

**"But not enough to say it is important on a $0.5T scale.**

**Insufficient."**

To be sure, there is a great deal of hype in this market.

For every successful crypto-asset, there are several failures.

Scammers have a disproportionately harmful impact on the space as a whole.

According to Reuters, "Twitter Inc. will begin prohibiting cryptocurrency advertising... following Facebook and Google in a clampdown to prevent exposing possible fraud or big investment losses."

Additionally, the sector faces significant obstacles.

How are these technologies going to scale? What are the incumbents' reactions likely to be? What actions will governments and regulators take? We have grounds to assume that this business urgently needs solid regulation to safeguard investors and deter fraudsters, or at the very least hold them accountable for their crimes. Additionally, market participants must grasp the road rules to continue investing and developing in this technology.

On the other hand, ineffective restrictions (even when implemented with the greatest intentions) can have unforeseen consequences and hinder innovation. Multiple authorities with overlapping mandates are conveying contradictory messages in certain nations. Regulators are in a difficult situation. Certain countries, such as Switzerland and Singapore, have developed as attractive sites for businesses to establish and operate, resulting in beneficial economic benefits for the local economy. According to one (informal) estimate, three thousand employments have been generated in the so-called "Crypto Valley" surrounding Zug and Zurich in recent years. The Crypto Valley Association now has around 600 members. These countries, which are smaller and more agile, have capitalized on a new industry, albeit they remain the exception, not the rule. For the time being, the general lack of regulatory clarity has generated confusion.

We continue to perceive them as implementation roadblocks that must be addressed.

When we look past the excitement and hysteria (not to mention fear, uncertainty, and doubt), we find something important taking place.

Bitcoin was the first step in a protracted push to build a new Internet technological stack, allowing the first native digital means of value.

That is what Blockchain is, and it is only limited by human creativity.

Certain innovators have envisaged an entirely new asset class comprised of at least seven distinct types:

- Bitcoin, Zcash, Monero, and Dash are all examples of cryptocurrencies.

- Tokenized protocols (ether, ICON, Aion, COSMOS, and NEO)

- Tokens of utility (Golem, BAT, and Spank)

- Tokenized securities (crypto equities, crypto bonds)

- Tokens representing natural resources

- Collectibles based on cryptography (CryptoKitties, Rare Pepe)

- Cryptocurrency fiat currencies and stable coins (proposed Fedcoin, Singapore's Project Ubin, MakerDAO)

We see one of the biggest wealth transitions in human history as we transition from paper-based analog assets to digital ones.

To be sure, $265 billion is a large sum of money.

However, when it comes to all of the world's assets — from stocks, bonds, and mortgages to carbon, land, and water — we have just scratched the surface of what we can construct with crypto.

Is this all artificial?

Perhaps.

According to Joseph Lubin, CEO of Consensys and creator of Ethereum, "we will witness bubble after bubble in our market, each with higher highs and lower lows."

That, I believe, is logical. While some argue that the dot-com boom and crash was harmful, I would argue that it was artistically destructive." It may have affected those seeking a fast profit, but it weeded unsustainable business models and wasteful operations. Perhaps more significantly, talent migrated to this new sector of the economy, and the excitement of the Internet age spurred billions of dollars in new technological infrastructure investment.

However, Blockchain is fundamentally different from the Internet in two respects.

To begin, where the Internet was a free utility built by a diverse group of stakeholders, many of whom were volunteers with a little financial incentive, Blockchain provides enormous financial rewards for those who build successful, scalable, and widely used technology via the appreciation of underlying crypto assets.

The early Internet pioneers would very certainly have enjoyed some upside from developing a trillion-dollar service, but that was unthinkable.

Blockchain is unique in that inventors, and early adopters may participate directly and financially in the Internet's second-age evolution.

As a result, it is not a single blockchain but a swarm of competing, overlapping and complementing platforms driven by incentives.

Second, Blockchain addresses value-added businesses such as financial services and supply chains, far larger than information-based businesses like media and publishing. Thus, not only will the effect be higher, but also the collective value. Indeed, the excitement is evident. However, as the adage goes, sometimes we need a little irrational enthusiasm to construct the future.

## 5.2 How Blockchain Reinvented Financial Services

If you want to know about the power of Blockchain, let me give you an interesting scenario here. A Blockchain-equipped car could use cryptocurrency to pay for its fuel. In case of an accident, such a car can automatically contact an insurance company while sending accurate information about the accidental damage.

The global financial system daily transacts trillions of dollars, serves billions of people, and underpins a global economy worth more than $100 trillion. It is the world's most powerful industry, the bedrock of global capitalism, and its leaders are referred to as the Masters of the Universe. Yet, closer examination reveals a Rube Goldberg machine of erratic developments and odd inconsistencies. To begin, the machine has not been upgraded in a long time. Instead, new technology has been haphazardly glued onto older infrastructure. Consider a bank that offers Internet banking but continues to use paper checks and mainframe computers from the 1970s. When a Starbucks client swipes her credit card on a state-of-the-art card reader to purchase a large espresso, her money is routed via no fewer than five separate intermediaries before reaching Starbucks' bank account. The transaction clears in seconds but takes days to settle.

Then there are huge international corporations such as Apple or GE. They must keep hundreds of bank accounts in local currencies throughout the world to facilitate their operations.

When such a firm has to transfer money between two subsidiaries in two separate countries, the manager of one subsidiary sends a bank wire from his operation's bank account to the bank account of the other company.

These transfers are unnecessarily difficult and take days, if not weeks, to complete.

Neither subsidiary can utilize the money to fund operations or investment during that period, but the intermediaries can receive interest on the float.

"The introduction of technology effectively transformed paper-based procedures into semi-automated, semi-electronic processes, but the rationale remained paper-based," Vikram Pandit, former CEO of Citigroup, explained.

Around every corner, another odd paradox: Traders purchase and sell securities in nanoseconds on the world's stock markets; their trades clear quickly yet take three full days to settle.

Local governments engage no less than ten different agencies to facilitate the issuance of municipal bonds—advisers, lawyers, insurers, and bankers, among others.

A day laborer in Los Angeles cashes his paycheck at a money mart for a 4% fee and then walks over to a convenience store to wire money to his family in Guatemala. He is charged again for flat fees, exchange rates, and other hidden costs. Once his family has distributed the funds among its numerous members, none has enough to establish a bank account or obtain credit.

They are among the 2.2 billion individuals who survive on less than $2 each day. The payments they require are minuscule, too small for conventional payment networks such as debit and credit cards, whose minimum costs prevent so-called micropayments.

According to a recent Harvard Business School research, banks do not regard providing these individuals as a "profitable proposition." As a result, the money machine is not genuinely global in breadth or scale.

Monetary policymakers and financial regulators frequently lack all the data due to the deliberate obscurity of many large financial operations and the compartmentalization of monitoring.

The global financial crisis of 2008 exemplified this idea.

Excessive leverage, a lack of transparency, and a sense of complacency fueled by warped incentives all contributed to no one spotting the problem until it was nearly too late.

"How can anything function, from a police force to a monetary system, without numbers and locations?" questioned Hernando de Soto.

Regulators are still attempting to govern this machine using industrial-era norms.

In New York State, money transmission regulations trace back to the Civil War, when the predominant mode of money transportation was horse and buggy.

Why, for example, does Western Union require 500,000 points of sale worldwide when more than half of the world's population owns a smartphone?

Erik Voorhees, a pioneer of bitcoin and outspoken opponent of the banking system, once told us, "It is faster to mail an anvil to China than it is to move money through the banking system."

That is insane!

Money is already digital; they are not transporting pallets of cash when you do a wire transfer!"

## Why is it so ineffective?

According to Paul David, the economist who coined the term "productivity paradox," building new technologies on top of existing infrastructure is "not uncommon during historical shifts from one technology paradigm to the next."

For example, manufacturers took forty years to accept commercial electrification over steam power, and frequently the two technologies coexisted until manufacturers finally made the switch permanently.

Productivity fell during the retrofitting period.

However, in the financial system, the problem is exacerbated by the lack of a seamless transition from one technology to the next; there are numerous legacy systems, some hundreds of years old, that never fully live up to their full potential.

**How come?** In part because finance is a monopolistic industry.

Nobel laureate Joseph Stiglitz stated in his assessment of the financial crisis that banks "were doing everything necessary to increase transaction costs in every way possible."

He contended that payments for actual products and services, even at the retail level, "should cost a fraction of a penny."

"However, how much do they charge?" he inquired.

"One, two, or three percent of the value of the item sold, whichever is greater. Capital and sheer scale, combined with a governmental and societal license to operate, enable banks to extract as much as possible in the country after country, most notably in the United States, earning billions of dollars." The possibility for huge centralized intermediates has always been substantial.

Not only traditional banks (e.g., Bank of America), but also charge card companies (Visa), investment banks (Goldman Sachs), stock exchanges (NYSE), clearinghouses (CME), wire/remittance services (Western Union), insurers (Lloyd's), securities law firms (Skadden, Arps), central banks (Federal Reserve), and asset management firms (Morgan Stanley).

This colossal behemoth is comprised of asset managers (BlackRock), accounting firms (Deloitte), consulting firms (Accenture), and commodities dealers (Vitol Group).

The financial system's gears—powerful middlemen that accumulate wealth and influence and frequently enforce monopoly economics—keep the system running but also slow it down, add expense, and generate disproportionate profits for themselves. Many incumbents have no incentive to improve products, increase efficiency, enhance the consumer experience, or appeal to the next generation due to their dominant position.

## A new look for the second-oldest profession in the world

The era of Franken-finance is drawing to a close, as blockchain technology promises to usher in a decade of significant upheaval and dislocation, but also huge potential for those who take it.

Today's global financial services industry is riddled with difficulties:

- It is archaic, constructed on decades-old technology incompatible with today's quickly evolving digital environment, making it frequently slow and unreliable.

- It is exclusive, depriving billions of people of essential financial instruments.

- It is centralized, which exposes it to data breaches, various types of threats, and outright failure.

Furthermore, it is monopolistic, perpetuating the existing quo and suffocating innovation.

Blockchain technology can solve all of these issues and many more as inventors and entrepreneurs discover new methods to create value on this robust platform.

# 5.3 How is Blockchain a Revolution?

Michael goes to the supermarket to shop but finds that his credit card is not working. Michael learns that his bank is facing a major computer meltdown, so none of its customers, including Michael, can make any payment. However, had the Blockchain technology been there, Michael would have been able to make payment even with his bank's system down. The Blockchain acts as a ledger that has a universal record of every Bitcoin transaction.

Michael's scenario is just one instance of how Blockchain is attempting to revolutionize the traditional economic system.

There are six primary reasons why blockchain technology will fundamentally alter this business, dismantling the finance monopoly and providing individuals and organizations with a real choice in creating and managing assets. Global industry participants should take note.

1. **Attestation:**

    For the first time in history, two parties who do not know or trust one another can transact and conduct business. As a result, verifying identity and building trust are no longer the financial intermediary's right and privilege. Additionally, in financial services, the term "trust protocol" has a double connotation. Additionally, the Blockchain may establish trust when it is required by authenticating any counterparty's identity and capacity using a combination of historical transaction history (on the Blockchain), reputation rankings based on aggregated evaluations, and other social and economic factors.

Additionally, the Blockchain may establish trust when it is required by authenticating any counterparty's identity and capacity using a combination of historical transaction history (on the Blockchain), reputation rankings based on aggregated evaluations, and other social and economic factors.

2. **Cost:**

On the Blockchain, the network clears and settles peer-to-peer value transfers continuously, ensuring that its ledger is always up to date.

To begin, banks could reduce an estimated $20 billion in back-office expenses without altering their basic business model, according to the Spanish bank Santander. Still, the true figure is almost certainly far higher.

With significantly lower costs, banks may provide consumers and businesses in underserved locations with increased access to financial services, markets, and financing. This can be beneficial not only to incumbents but also to scrappy upstarts and entrepreneurs worldwide. Anyone, everywhere, with a smartphone and an Internet connection, can tap into the huge veins of global finance.

3. **Speed:**

Today, remittances settle in three to seven days. Stock trades settle in two to three days, whereas bank loan trades take an average of twenty-three days to settle.

The SWIFT network processes fifteen million payment orders every day between ten thousand financial institutions worldwide, but they take days to clear and settle.

The same is true for the Automated Clearing House (ACH) system, which processes trillions of dollars in payments in the United States each year.

The bitcoin network clears and settles all transactions that occur during that period in an average of ten minutes.

Other blockchain networks are much faster. New inventions such as the Bitcoin Lightning Network seek to rapidly extend the bitcoin blockchain's capacity while reducing settlement and clearing times to a fraction of a second.

"In the equivalent financial world, when a sender is located in one network, and a receiver is located in another, transactions must pass via several ledgers, many intermediaries, and several hops.

Things can go wrong in the middle. There are numerous capital requirements for that," Ripple Labs CEO Chris Larsen stated.

Indeed, the transition to rapid and frictionless value transmission would liberate wealth previously imprisoned in transit, which would be terrible news for anyone earning from the float.

4. **Risk Mitigation:**

The first is settlement risk or the possibility that your deal will reverse course due to a hiccup in the settlement procedure. The second type of risk is counterparty risk or the possibility that your counterparty will default before settling a contract. The most significant risk is systemic risk, calculated as the sum of all outstanding counterparty risk in the system. Vikram Pandit coined the term "Herstatt risk" after a German bank that failed to satisfy its obligations and ultimately went bankrupt: "We discovered during the financial crisis that one of the risks was if I'm trading with someone, how do I know that they are going to settle on the other side?" According to Pandit, a fast settlement on the Blockchain might fully eliminate this danger. Accountants could peer into the inner workings of a business at any point in time and see which transactions were taking place and how the network recorded them. In addition, the irreversibility of a transaction and quick reconciliation of financial reporting would eliminate one part of agency risk — the possibility that unscrupulous managers would use the lengthy paper trail and large time delay to conceal misconduct.

5. **Value innovation:**

The bitcoin blockchain was created to exchange bitcoins, not to store other financial assets. The technology, on the other hand, is open source, which encourages experimentation. Certain entrepreneurs are constructing their blockchains, dubbed altcoins, for purposes other than bitcoin payments.

Others are leveraging the bitcoin blockchain's size and liquidity to create "spin-off" coins on so-called sidechains that can be "colored" to represent any physical or digital asset or liability—a corporate stock or bond, a barrel of oil, a bar of gold, a car, a car payment, a receivable or a payable, or, of course, a currency.

Sidechains are blockchains that are distinct from the bitcoin blockchain in terms of features and functionality, but harness bitcoin's established network and hardware infrastructure without jeopardizing its security characteristics.

Sidechains communicate with the Blockchain via a two-way peg, a cryptographic mechanism for transferring the Blockchain and back assets without using a third-party exchange. Others are attempting to eliminate the coin or token by developing trading platforms on private blockchains.

Financial institutions are already utilizing blockchain technology to record, exchange, and trade assets and liabilities. It can eventually replace traditional exchanges and centralized markets, fundamentally altering how value is defined and traded.

6. **Open Source:**

   The financial services industry has a technology stack of legacy systems twenty miles tall and on the edge of collapsing. Also, change is challenging since any improvement must be backward compatible. As an open-source technology, Blockchain may constantly evolve, evolve, and develop depending on network consensus.

These benefits — attestation, dramatically lower costs, lightning-fast processing, reduced risk, great value innovation, and adaptability — have the potential to transform not only payments but also the securities industry, investment banking, accounting and auditing, venture capital, insurance, enterprise risk management, retail banking, and other industry pillars.

# 5.4 From Stock Exchanges to Block Exchanges

"Wall Street has awoken hugely," Blockstream's Austin Hill observed.

He was referring to the financial sector's intense interest in blockchain technology. Consider the case of Blythe Masters, one of Wall Street's most influential women. She transformed JPMorgan's derivatives and commodities department into a global powerhouse and helped pioneer the derivatives market. Following a temporary pseudo retirement, she became CEO of Digital Asset Holdings, a New York-based start-up. Many were taken aback by the conclusion. She saw that the Blockchain would alter her business in the same way that the Internet did for other industries: "I would take it about as seriously as you should have taken the Internet notion in the 1990s." This is a significant event that will alter the way our financial system operates."

Masters had ignored several early accounts of bitcoin being abused by drug traffickers, controlled by gamblers, and heralded by libertarians as ushering in a new global order.

Late in 2014, this changed.

Masters explained, "I had an 'aha moment' in which I saw the technology's potential consequences for the world I was familiar with."

While the distributed ledgers technology's application to bitcoin was intriguing and had ramifications for payments, the underlying database technology had much larger ramifications." According to Masters, blockchain technology has the potential to cut inefficiencies and costs by allowing many parties to rely on the same information rather than duplicating and copying it and then reconciling it. As a result, blockchain is the "golden source" because it enables shared, decentralized, replicated transaction records.

"Keep in mind that the infrastructures supporting financial services have remained mostly unchanged for decades.

While the front end has developed, the back end has remained static," Masters explains.

"There has been an arms race in technological investment focused on transaction processing speed, to the point that competitive advantages are now measured in fractions of nanoseconds.

The irony is that post-trade infrastructure has remained essentially unchanged.

It still takes "days, if not weeks," to complete the post-trade procedure necessary for actually settling and recording financial transactions.

Masters' excitement for blockchain technology is not unique.

"I am a firm believer in blockchain technology's power to fundamentally alter the financial services industry's infrastructure," NASDAQ CEO Bob Greifeld stated.

Greifeld is integrating distributed ledger technology from Blockchain into NASDAQ's private markets platform, dubbed NASDAQ Linq.

Exchanges are controlled markets for securities and are therefore susceptible to disruption.

NASDAQ Linq executed its first blockchain transaction on January 1, 2016.

According to Hill, one of the world's top asset managers committed more resources to its blockchain innovation division than we do to our entire organization.

Hill's business has raised more than $75 million and employs over twenty individuals.

"These men are committed to ensuring that they understand how technology can be used to transform their businesses."

The New York Stock Exchange, Goldman Sachs, Santander, Deloitte, RBC, Barclays, and UBS, to name a few, have all expressed a comparable level of serious interest.

In 2015, Wall Street's view of blockchain technology became unanimously favorable: 94 percent of respondents in one research agreed that blockchain technology might play a significant role in finance.

Although numerous other applications pique Wall Street's interest, what interests financial executives worldwide is the prospect of using the Blockchain to securely process any trade from start to finish, significantly lowering costs, increasing speed and efficiency, and mitigating risk in their businesses.

According to Blythe Masters, the entire life cycle of a trade, including its execution, the netting of multiple trades against one another, and the reconciliation of who did what with whom and whether they agree, can occur at the trade entry-level, much earlier in the stack of processes than in the traditional financial market. Greifeld stated as follows: "At the moment, we settle deals on a T+3 basis (three days). Why not take five or ten minutes to settle?"

Wall Street is a risk-taking institution, and this technology can significantly decrease counterparty risk, settlement risk, and systemic risk across the system.

According to Jesse McWaters, the World Economic Forum's financial innovation head, "The most intriguing aspect of distributed ledger technology is the potential for systemic stability to be improved."

He feels that these "new technologies enable regulators to be more lenient."

Due to the public character of the Blockchain—its openness and searchability—along with its automatic settlement and unchangeable time stamps, regulators may monitor activity and even set up alerts to ensure they don't miss anything.

# Chapter 6: Conducting the Business

When I deliver lectures to my students, I prefer to go in a specific sequence. Surely, the sequence and order play a great role in how you grasp ideas and concepts better. Therefore, I am using the same sequence of topics in this book as I use for my students in class. For now, we have learned enough about Blockchain. Now let us take a break and move to the trading and mining part. After this part, we will take a step back and discuss more about blockchain to have a strong grasp of the concept. In the final part of this chapter, we will discuss what crypto exchanges are and how you should store your crypto assets. I hope you will enjoy this sequence.

## 6.1 Crypto Trading

While hearing the term "trading," you could imagine that not everyone is capable of mastering this job. You are partially correct. However, you will succeed if you have a basic understanding of the trade, are interested in economic news and events, and keep an eye on the exchange rate. You might even learn how to construct financial forecasts.

Indeed, trading on a cryptocurrency exchange is very similar to trading on a stock exchange.

It is simply necessary to understand how to examine charts, make sound judgments, avoid pandering to fear, gossip, or emotions, and, most importantly, to be prepared to lose everything.

I have a friend, William, who switched to crypto trading some years after me. A few years back, when I met him on my visit to Canada, he was upset because his crypto trading was not rewarding him as he had expected. After learning more about the matter, I realized a few things.

- William wanted to see huge gains on his crypto portfolio overnight. He wanted to succeed, but he wanted to succeed "right now!"

- He lacked a precise plan while entering the crypto market.

After realizing the above points, I told William a few things.

"Look, my friend. The Crypto market is uncertain. It is somewhat unrealistic to get away from the highs and lows of something before you get to see the success. After all, the darkest hour is just before dawn. So, you have to be patient. First, you need to observe the price trends closely. And then, you should work your way up accordingly."

I further told my friend that a good step-by-step plan is helpful when it comes to crypto trading. Just as the famous saying goes, "Failing to plan is planning to fail." This is very much applicable in crypto as well. Also, when it comes to emotional factors, you have to avoid fear and greed.

Now, an incredible piece of motivation for all my readers lies in this part of the story. Today, not only is William making excellent profits on his Bitcoins, but he is also planning to collaborate with the concerned organizations to promote awareness about cryptocurrencies and Bitcoins. Inspirational, right? Tomorrow, you could also be an inspiration, just like my friend William.

The stock market is based on the exchange of currency pairings.

Each transaction side establishes its terms, and the other party chooses whether to accept them or not.

On a bitcoin exchange, you operate exclusively with buying and selling orders. By placing an order, you can specify a lower or greater price than the currently available price.

You choose the number of coins you wish to purchase and your desired price. If the market meets your quoted price, your order is filled.

Allow me to clarify when you can make an order on a cryptocurrency exchange. Assume that you read in the news that Bitcoin prices will decrease and then rise again. Now is the time to invest. I want to emphasize, however, that there is no precise method for determining which currencies to invest in and when. The critical point is to avoid investing in a coin at its highest price. On the contrary, it is prudent to buy in coins at the outset of recovery following a drawdown and, of course, in stable-growing coins.

Let us take an example here for a better understanding. Linda wants to invest in cryptocurrency. However, she is not sure which currency will be most suitable to invest in. Linda's good friend, Mary, has suggested her to invest in Bitcoin. Marry knows that the Bitcoin price skyrocketed back in 2020. Although there have been some wild speculations about the Bitcoin price trends and Bitcoin bubble lately in 2021, Marry still thinks that Bitcoin is a worthwhile investment. "This is because I have looked at Bitcoin's history. If we study the last five years' Bitcoin price data, its price has bounced back after every crash. Therefore, Bitcoin has had a consistent outperformance so far. So, it is still a popular investment opportunity." Marry educates Linda on the matter.

Marry is right when she looks at Bitcoin's history while providing facts to Linda. However, there is another factor that Linda will need to consider while investing. Linda needs to make sure that she does not invest in Bitcoin when its price is at its best. That way, if the price is low at the time of investment, there will be some good chances for a spike in the coming days. That's how it works.

Consider and study the market carefully while selecting coins for trading. Additionally, keep an eye out for news on the release of new coins and monitor the price charts of major coins.

Another critical issue is that you must know when to buy or sell to benefit. If you make a mistake, you have a good possibility of transitioning from a being short-term investor to a long-term strategic investor. Bear in mind the exchange fees. Additionally, I want to remind you to invest just the amount of money you are willing to lose.

You must never borrow money to trade in the market. You will inevitably lose money in this market. Therefore, security is a vital component of trading. Security is critical in every sector that involves money.

Even more so in the cryptocurrency market, where the value of your investment portfolio can easily exceed many tens of thousands of dollars, it would be irresponsible not to consider security in advance.

It would be best if you investigate all possible safeguards for your financial security.

**Which method is the most convenient for stealing your cryptocurrency?**

The answer is straightforward: to take it from the stock exchange.

Allow me to illustrate.

In the summer of 2017, South Korea's largest cryptocurrency exchange, Bithumb, reported billions of dollars in losses due to hacking.

That is why, I believe that maintaining funds on the exchange is dangerous. The advantages of hot wallets stored on the exchange are their accessibility and speed of operation. In addition, they are easily accessible since they are connected to the Internet.

However, hot wallets have a significant disadvantage in terms of susceptibility due to their Internet connection.

I will not elaborate further on trading here since I have dedicated an entire book on trading as one of the most popular methods of profiting in the cryptocurrency market.

## 6.2 Crypto Mining

The term mining was coined about gold mining. Mining is the process of creating new cryptocurrencies, such as Bitcoins. Miners are those who own or operate mining devices. Often, the term "miner" refers to the computational device required to identify Bitcoin (or another cryptocurrency) in the network.

Mining is accomplished by deciphering a block's digital signature.

A block is an array of data providing information on transactions in the Bitcoin network after the previous block was produced.

A network participant who successfully deciphers the digital signature is rewarded with bitcoin.

Simultaneously, to obtain a "gold bar" in the form of a precious generating transaction, a miner must sift through tonnes of "dead rock," i.e., hashes inappropriate for the block.

Thus, each new block has a digital signature that is derived from the previous block. The blocks stick to one another and form a chain of blocks dubbed the Blockchain.

The majority of people believe that mining is money generated by an electrical outlet. However, it is an excellent piece of meticulous effort that is rewarded with money by the system.

Even though both the client code and the bitcoin protocol code are completely open, generating new coins is time-consuming and costly. For instance, you cannot generate more bitcoins than the technology's designer intended. Large investments in equipment, buildings, cooling systems, and electricity are required to acquire new coins. That is why Bitcoin is referred to as "digital gold" and is presented like gold coins.

Now, let us address the following question: Why does cryptocurrency require miners?

There is a widespread misperception that miners created cryptocurrencies. Indeed, miners manage the network's critical functions:

- Transaction confirmation.
- Protection of the network from erroneous data entry (false transactions and blocks).
- Protection of the network from a variety of attacks.
- Decentralization of the network must be maintained.

That is why the more mining devices on the network, the more secure the Bitcoin network is against attacks. Simultaneously, shutting off a portion of its computation capacity will not interrupt network transactions.

The network will continue to operate as long as at least one miner is active. To date, mining has been conducted using specialized ASIC or GPU (graphics processing unit) chips.

ASIC is a computer chip designed exclusively for mining. It is a "soulless robot" that has been programmed to extract cryptocurrency. In terms of GPU mining, a typical farm comprises numerous video cards of the same brand, a powerful power supply, a motherboard with multiple PCI-Express slots, and a processor with a cooling system.

Coins operate according to specific algorithms. Therefore, you should choose video cards based on these algorithms.

### Which is better for mining: ASIC or GPU?

ASIC is simple to service and install. However, it is designed to work with a limited number of coins and will not allow you to switch between them.

If you pick ASIC, you will need to mine successfully enough to cover your electricity expenses, as you would require a large amount of electrical equipment. In comparison to ASIC, you can quickly and profitably sell your video card if you decide to stop mining at some point.

I believe that mining requires both ASIC and GPU hardware. If one of the devices fails, the second one can be used. There is another option for those who are not interested in creating a "money machine." You can mine remotely by pooling processing power. This is referred to as cloud mining.

However, you should be aware of the risks associated with cloud mining. To begin, the payback period is rather misleading. Second, you have no control over spending or earnings. Additionally, none of the equipment is your property.

If you decide to outsource mining, keep the following in mind: you should not be offered an exorbitant profit forecast, and you should have access to technical help.

Additionally, I recommend that you study reviews and follow mining forums regarding these companies and invest modest sums of money for testing purposes before investing more money.

As with trading, certain security regulations apply to mining. For example, the first rule of the so-called "mining club" is to keep the location of your mining rigs a secret.

Is this a trivial point? You may believe so.

However, keep in mind that you must be the only person with access to the premises and your mining equipment.

## 6.3 Getting A Better Understanding of Blockchain

Individuals began utilizing Blockchain technology for non-cryptocurrency-related objectives. As a result, they obtained a greater grasp of how it operates, including data storage for valuables, identities, contracts, and property rights, among other things. Ethereum is the most detailed blockchain creation to date, and it is a primary emphasis of the book. Similar to cloud computing applications, various kinds of categories of Blockchain have emerged. As with the cloud, there are three types of blockchains: public blockchains that anyone can access and update, private blockchains that only a little community within a firm can access and update, and the third type of blockchain consortium works collaboratively. For example, while working on Wall Street, we witnessed a consortium created by five of the largest investment banking firms. Due to the consortium's institutional role in facilitating trades among its members, it is envisaged that Blockchain as a financial technology tool would emerge in this manner. Each blockchain type is covered briefly in the sections below.

## Public Blockchains

A public blockchain is one that its authors envision as the following: a blockchain that anyone can access and engage with, a blockchain that only includes valid transactions, and a blockchain in which anyone can participate in the consensus phase. As previously stated, the consensus method determines which blocks are added to the chain and its present state. Rather than relying on a central node, the public Blockchain is secured through cryptographic authentication and mining incentives. Anyone may serve as a miner by compiling and publishing those transactions. Because no user is inherently trusted to verify transactions on the public Blockchain, all users must adhere to an algorithm that verifies transactions through the use of software and hardware resources to brute-force solve an issue (i.e., by solving the cryptographic puzzle). The miner who discovers the solution first gets rewarded, and each new solution, combined with the transactions that authenticate it, becomes the basis for the next challenge to be solved. Thus, the authentication principles are proof-of-work and proof-of-stake.

## Blockchains in a Consortium

A consortium blockchain, such as R3 (www.r3cev.com), is a distributed ledger in which a pre-selected group of nodes manages the consensus mechanism—for example, a consortium of nine financial institutions, each of which operates a node, and of which five (including the US Supreme Court) must sign each block for the block to be legitimate. The ability to read the Blockchain can be made public or restricted to participants, and there are also hybrid options, such as making the block's root hashes public and providing a public API that enables members of the public to make a limited number of queries and obtain cryptographic proofs of certain parts of the blockchain state. Thus, blockchains are distributed ledgers that are "partially decentralized."

## Private Blockchains

A truly private blockchain is one in which all write permissions are concentrated in the hands of a single person. Read permissions can be adjusted to be public or limited to a certain extent. Because database administration and internal auditing inside a single company are both possible uses, wide readability may be unnecessary in some circumstances, while public auditing may be required in others. In addition, private blockchains may be used to build compliance agents for regulations such as HIPAA (Health Insurance Portability and Accountability Act), anti-money laundering (AML), and know-your-customer (KYC) rules.

## Comparison of the various types:

In a recent class, I was discussing the concept of blockchains with my students. We talked about various types when one of the students inquired if it was true that a vast majority preferred private blockchains over other types. I assume that to set a priority for Blockchain types, understanding the distinctions between public, consortium, and private blockchains is critical. Therefore, even those who favor a centralized structure over a distributed ledger receive a cryptographic audit.

In comparison to public blockchains, private blockchains offer several benefits. A private blockchain user can modify the Blockchain's rules. Financial partners who use a blockchain will be able to amend transactions if errors are discovered. They will still be able to rebalance the universe and wipe everything clean.

There is, however, a trail. In some circumstances, this function is required, such as when an erroneous transaction is released or a vicious form gains access and becomes the new owner, as is the case with the property registry.

This is also valid on a public blockchain if the government possesses backdoor access keys, as they did under the Clinton era. On the private Blockchain, transactions are less expensive because they are only verified by a few trusted nodes with a lot of computer power. Although public blockchains currently charge greater transaction fees, this will change as new scaling breakthroughs reduce public blockchain costs and enable the development of a more robust blockchain framework.

Nodes can be trusted to be exceptionally well connected, and errors may quickly be repaired manually, allowing the use of consensus techniques that achieve finality in very shorter block durations. In addition, public blockchain technology advancements, such as Ethereum's proof-of-stake mechanism, will bring public blockchains closer to the ideal of "instant confirmation." Private blockchains, on the other hand, will remain faster, and the latency difference will never disappear entirely since, unfortunately, the speed of light does not double every two years, as Moore's law implies. Furthermore, if read rights are limited, private blockchains can give a better level of privacy.

In light of this, private blockchains may appear to be a superior alternative for organizations. On the other hand, public blockchains are critical in an institutional setting. In truth, this value is founded on the philosophical ideals championed by proponents of public blockchains for years, the most important of which are equality, neutrality, and transparency. The benefits of public blockchains can be classified into two categories:

- Public blockchains enable app users to be protected from developers by demonstrating that such acts are beyond the control of the app creators.

- Because public blockchains are available for the public, they can be used by a wide variety of organizations, resulting in certain networking benefits. For example, we can reduce expenses to near-zero with a smart contract if we have asset-holding schemes on a blockchain and a currency on the same Blockchain. Party A can transmit the asset to a program, which will transmit it automatically to Party B, who will pay the program, and the program is trusted since it runs on a public blockchain. Take note that for this to operate well, two very dissimilar asset groupings from very different industries must be stored in the same database. Additionally, other asset owners, such as land registries and title insurance companies, may utilize this.

## 6.4 The Game Theory

The term "game theory" refers to a body of theory about games not confined to children's games. Almost often, two or more parties are engaged in some form of strategic action. For example, a cricket tournament is a game of competition. There are two opposing parties in a court of law surrounded by lawyers and juries, two siblings squabbling over ice cream, a political election, and a traffic signal. Another illustration: Assume you applied for a blockchain job and were picked and offered pay but declined the offer because you believed that there was a significant demand-supply gap and that the offer would be updated to include a greater salary. What, you may ask, isn't a game? Almost everything in real life is a game. As a result, a "game" might be defined as a situation that requires making a "correlated rational option." This indicates that a player's prospects are influenced by their own decisions and others in a similar situation. In other words, if the decisions of others affect your destiny, you are participating in a game. So, what is game theory?

Game theory is the study of complex game strategies. It is the art of making the best decision or selecting the most appropriate method in a particular situation based on the goal. To accomplish so, one must first know the opponent's plan and his or her assessment of your next move. Consider the following example: Two brothers and sisters, the eldest being the elder and the youngest being the younger. There are two types of ice cream in the refrigerator: one is orange, and the other is mango. The elder desires to consume the orange flavor, but he is aware that the younger will scream for the same orange. As a result, he opts for the mango-flavored ice cream, which his younger sibling copies. The elder one pretends to have sacrificed the mango-flavored ice cream and offers it to the younger one while consuming the orange one. Kindly take the situation. It is a win-win situation for both parties, which was the elder's goal. If the elder had chosen to do so, he might have clashed with the younger and obtained the orange one. In the second scenario, the elder child must plan when to strike so that the younger child is not mortally hurt but is frightened enough to relinquish the orange-flavored ice cream. This is game theory in action: what is your goal, and what is the optimal line of action?

Another illustration, this time from a business perspective: Assume you are a vendor selling veggies in a certain location. There are three routes to town, one of which is considered the standard way because everyone takes it, probably because it is shorter and more convenient. You discover that your usual route has been closed one day due to maintenance work, and you cannot use it.

There are now only two options available to you. One of them is a brief but winding journey to the desired area. The alternative is a somewhat longer but still good route. You must develop a plan to determine which of the two routes to take. Highways may be congested, and many drivers will take the shortest route.

This could result in severe traffic congestion on that stretch of the route, causing substantial delays. Thus, to take in town on time, you chose the longer route, but at the cost of a few extra dollars spent on gas. You are convinced that you will easily compensate if you arrive on time and sell your vegetables fairly. This is what game theory is all about: determining the optimal course of action to accomplish your objective, often finding the best solution.

In some cases, the role you play and the goal you wish to achieve are also critical considerations when designing a plan. For instance, if you are the host of a sporting event rather than a competitor, you will design a plan to ensure that participants play the rules and procedures. This is because, as an organizer, you are unconcerned with the outcome. On the other hand, a participant will plan winning movements considering the opponent's strengths and weaknesses and the organizer's rules, as violating the rules may result in fines. Assume for a moment that you are the organizer in this case. Then, consider the scenario wherein a competitor violates a regulation and is penalized one point but injures their opponent to the point where they cannot play. As a result, you must consider the players' perspectives and modify your rules appropriately.

Let us attempt to describe game theory once again using the knowledge gained from the previous examples. It is a technique for recreating real-world scenarios in a game and determining the optimal strategy or move for an individual or an object in a particular situation to achieve the desired outcome.

Politics, social media, community planning, bidding, betting, marketing, distributed storage, distributed computing, supply chains, and finance are just a few of the applications of game theory ideas.

It is feasible to create frameworks based on game theory in which players adhere to the rules without assuming emotional or moral values. If you want to move beyond just generating a proof of concept and bring the product or solution to market, game theory should be regarded as one of the most crucial parts. It will assist you in developing robust solutions and validating them against many intriguing scenarios. For example, many people think in game-theoretic terms without even realizing it. However, it does help if you have access to the numerous resources and tactics made available by game theory.

## What Is the Point of Studying Game Theory?

Game theory is a ground-breaking multidisciplinary phenomenon that bridges psychology, economics, mathematics, philosophy, and various other academic fields.

Theoretically, game theory is said to apply to real-world problems. But, on the other hand, the issues are limitless. Are game-theoretic concepts still infinite? Certainly! Whether we are aware of it or not, we apply game theory daily, and we frequently utilize our brains to identify the best course of action in a particular situation. We are, aren't we? If such is the case, what point does understanding game theory serve?

There are numerous examples in game theory that can help us think differently. Numerous real-world scenarios have been devised and applied to certain theories, such as Nash Equilibrium.

In some real-world situations, participants or players face a decision matrix approaching a "prisoner's dilemma." By mastering these ideas, one may formulate questions more mathematically and arrive at the correct decision.

It enables us to identify variables that each participant should consider before deciding on a course of action in a particular interaction.

To take the appropriate action, it is necessary first to identify the type of game, who the players are, their objectives or goals, and possible acts. Numerous real-world decisions include multiple parties. Game theory is the theoretical underpinning of rational decision-making.

The Byzantine Generals' Dilemma is frequently used to assure data consistency between compute nodes in distributed storage solutions and data centers.

## 6.5 Cryptocurrency Exchanges

Several cryptocurrency exchanges are accessible, which means that everyone has a chance to pick one that meets their specific demands. With that in mind, I would want to address some concerns about bitcoin exchange registration.

I will provide you with a broader picture here. Richard is an amateur in crypto trading. Initially, when he started, he did not have much awareness about crypto exchanges. Due to a lack of much-needed care and other important know-how, Richard's crypto wallet got hacked. Although he lost only a few hundred dollars, if measured in today's terms, he still realized that a few vital strategies need to be followed when registering in a crypto exchange. Richard then implemented various methods along with the cold storage, and now his wallet is safe.

When registering on an exchange, I strongly advise you to enable two-factor authentication (identification). Even if you are already registered, I strongly advise you to utilize this. In addition, I recommend that you open accounts on at least two exchanges; if something happens to one, you will be able to cancel the orders on the other.

Your password must contain at least ten characters in each of the following categories: uppercase letters, lowercase letters, and numerals.

Do not expect to remember it even if it is the simplest possible combination of letters. As a result, ensure that you write it down and save it safely. You may even have a password tattoo, but it must be written down someplace, either on your body or on paper!

The second restriction is that you may not use this password for any purpose other than the exchange. You must have a unique e-mail address for each exchange account. If one of your e-mail accounts is compromised and hackers attempt to access your account on the exchange, your other account will remain secure.

Do not forget to check your e-mail while making a deposit or withdrawal from the exchange. These transactions require confirmation by e-mail.

Finally, if you take the risk of trading on a cryptocurrency exchange, you must be prepared for the possibility that a hacker (or even the exchange owner) may steal your money at any time.

Any exchange is also susceptible to failure. As a result, holding money on the exchange is extremely risky. Therefore, I encourage you to maintain just the funds you use to trade on the exchange and save the remainder in cold wallets.

## 6.6 Cold Storage

Assuming you are interested in properly storing your crypto assets, I will discuss cold storage in greater detail.

Cold storage is a word that refers to private keys that are often generated and stored in a safe, isolated environment. This means that your funds will not be stored on any website. This wallet resembles a USB flash drive: you can attach it to a computer and conduct a transaction instantly.

Trezor, KeepKey, and Ledger are the most popular cold storage wallets. This is a fairly popular approach for keeping a large amount of Bitcoin. Transactions are infrequent, and security is a top priority.

As a result, cold storage is the best option if you intend to keep your cash for an extended period.

There is another secure method of storing your cryptocurrency — Bitcoin debit cards. The essence of these cards is likewise pretty straightforward. First, you create an account on the site and fund it with bitcoins. Following that, the service transfers your Bitcoin debit card, tied to your mobile phone number, to the specified address. It is quite convenient to pay for things with this card. However, I must tell you that this type of store is not inexpensive. Each time you use this card, you will be charged a cost of around 3%.

As a result, this technique of Bitcoin storage is not suitable for regular use. However, this card is ideal for individuals who receive their wage in Bitcoin and wish to use it to make transactions anywhere in the world.

Finally, keep in mind that a wallet can be hacked, which means that any hot storage option has some risk. Also, avoid storing all of your money on a single card.

You will need hot wallets to fund your bitcoin exchange account and conduct transactions. They are also utilized to participate in the initial coin offering (ICO). However, I recommend that you keep the majority of your money in a cold wallet.

Because it is not connected to the Internet, it cannot be hacked, making it significantly more secure.

To ensure the security of your wallet, create a unique e-mail account for each, encrypt it with two-factor authentication, and, most importantly, write down all your passwords on paper.

# Chapter 7: The Future of Cryptocurrency

You have reached the last chapter of this book. By now, you must have many ideas about cryptocurrencies in your mind. But you might just be wondering where to begin. I would suggest you observe the existing conditions and opportunities around you and then analyze where you stand. But after coming this far, are you just wondering if crypto trading is worth it? Are you curious about the future of cryptocurrency? Do you think that ever since its introduction to the world about a decade ago, cryptocurrency has made its mark with a groundbreaking innovation?

## 7.1 The Future of Bitcoin

Bitcoin's future appears to be both unforeseeable and unstoppable. Nobody knows for certain what will happen, but it appears as though Bitcoin has penetrated far enough into the mainstream that it cannot be reversed. Numerous major businesses, including airlines, technology businesses, government organizations, and the financial industry, have begun to embrace Bitcoin and, perhaps more significantly, the underlying blockchain technology. Moreover, the growing demand for skilled blockchain programmers across various businesses demonstrates the blockchain era.

A new generation of entrepreneurs has emerged in the cryptocurrency and blockchain area, inventing novel applications centered on Bitcoin as both a currency and a technology. Only time will tell if Bitcoin as a currency will continue to appreciate and continue to dominate the cryptocurrency markets or whether a disruptive upstart will dethrone it. Diversifying your cryptocurrency holdings is viewed as a technique to boost your chances of picking a winner by many.

Hearing stories about early Bitcoin adopters who made millions can make people to Bitcoin feel as if they are too late. While it is unknown whether Bitcoin will be the "one coin to rule them all," the promise of blockchain technology is only just beginning to gain traction in the mainstream, bubbling to the surface of a vast sea of possibility. No crystal ball can reveal the precise shape of the future, but one thing is certain: this is only the beginning. Five or ten years from now, people who invest prudent investments today may very well be considered "early adopters."

## 7.2 The Future of Ethereum

Ether's value reached all-time highs in 2021, and many believe that the value will continue to rise over time. Numerous large companies have embraced Ethereum's promise of a scalable blockchain platform capable of executing smart contracts. As the promise of blockchain technology becomes more apparent on a global scale, a wave of entrepreneurs has emerged to incorporate it into every field of technology, from energy to healthcare to politics.

It remains to be seen whether the Ethereum platform will ultimately become the de facto foundation for developing decentralized blockchain apps. Ethereum could be compared to an early web browser such as Netscape Navigator, and some future attempt could become the "Google of blockchain." Given the novelty of this technology, it would be naive to dismiss that possibility. But, of course, Ethereum may continue to grow, improve, and ultimately dominate this space. The imminent switch to the Casper algorithm and Proof-of-Stake will be a litmus test for Ethereum's ability to evolve.

Whether you intend to invest in Ether or another token produced via an Ethereum-based application, or you wish to develop your decentralized application on the Ethereum blockchain, it is critical to keep informed. Technology advances at a breakneck pace in this space, and when blockchain technology penetrates large businesses, we will certainly see changes in the way cryptocurrencies and blockchain applications are regulated. Joining online groups and conversations like Reddit, Slack channels, and Twitter is an excellent way to remain informed about Ethereum platform advancements. Learning about other platforms, reading whitepapers, and becoming acquainted with how leaders in this field can help you develop a broader perspective. A deeper understanding can help you formulate your own opinions about which technologies are likely to succeed and how to invest.

Of course, we cannot predict how the future will unfold. But, regardless of how the future unfolds, it is almost destined to be shaped by blockchain technology. Today, Ethereum represents one of the most established and forward-thinking approaches to making this technology accessible, adaptable, and exciting. As a result, the opportunities are limitless for investors, developers, and entrepreneurs in this cutting-edge space.

Let us look at a case scenario to understand how Ethereum can benefit enterprises. Robert is an entrepreneur in the finance sector. Recently, Robert shifted all of his company's transactions to Ethereum. He says that cryptocurrency helps in business payment settlements while maintaining high privacy and upgrading his business performance. In addition, Robert anticipates that the next decade will be an era of low-cost and high-speed payments due to the increased use of Ethereum and other such cryptocurrencies in businesses.

## 7.3 The Future of Blockchain

Throughout this book, we have discussed various fundamental principles relating to blockchain technology. As the world becomes more connected via networked technology and the amount of data we generate increases quantity and quality, there is a rising demand and opportunity for new organizational structures to manage the interface between digital and material life. The use of a distributed ledger in conjunction with the ability to create decentralized rather than hierarchical systems in a safe, trustless, and open manner is a significant step toward reinventing how many of today's dominating institutions operate.

As with any new technology, the blockchain ecosystem is characterized by opposing philosophies, disparate implementations, and a slew of obstacles. Only time will tell if the Bitcoin blockchain will remain the dominant blockchain model and Bitcoin will remain the most popular cryptocurrency. Without question, there is a tremendous opportunity for growth to reach the full potential of blockchain technology in terms of institutional transparency, decentralized networks, peer-to-peer transactions, and asset management, to name a few. Healthcare, banking, social media, and retail, aviation, and manufacturing have all begun to investigate the feasibility of integrating with blockchain-based systems. Governments, banks, and nonprofit groups have already begun implementing blockchain technology to govern transactions, public service access, and humanitarian aid distribution.

Executing transactions in a trustless environment without using a "middleman" is a basic tenet of blockchain technology. In layman's terms, we ultimately trust an unbiased mathematical process performed by computers rather than human individuals. As a result, we are assured of a level of security that is theoretically impervious to human meddling.

Of fact, it is difficult to disregard human beings fully. The strength of a decentralized application based on computational verification represents a paradigm shift away from a top-down structure and toward a distributed network. However, a closer examination of the Bitcoin blockchain reveals that the consensus model requires agreement by a majority to verify a block. A majority of miners (51%).

What if, as mining costs continue to rise in tandem with the ever-growing blockchain, miners consolidate their influence into ever-larger pools? This is not a purely theoretical matter. At the time of this writing, two big mining pools are expected to mine about 50% of all Bitcoin blocks.

To execute a so-called "51 percent attack," a single organization must provide at least 51% of the Bitcoin network's mining hash rate. This would take an almost unfathomable amount of computer power, equating to an equally unfathomable electrical cost. In reality, most governments lack the resources necessary to execute a 51 percent attack on Bitcoin. It would be extremely tough, but not impossible. If this were to occur, the attacker would be unable to gain complete control of the network. Instead, they would prevent new transactions from being validated but not reverse previously recorded transactions, take Bitcoins from other people's wallets, or produce new Bitcoins at will.


The 51% issue is one that any decentralized system created on a similar model would face. However, according to certain proponents of the Proof-of-Stake consensus, this model provides stronger security against a 51 percent attack.

Blockchains, like other burgeoning industries and new technologies, confronts obstacles. However, the blockchain space is generating a whole generation of entrepreneurs, developers, and experts. For those who believe in the transformative potential of this technology, it is a land of opportunity.

Whether you are intrigued by the ideological implications of decentralized networks fundamentally altering the landscape of hierarchical organizations on a global scale or are an investor looking for the next big thing, blockchain technology is undeniably intriguing. Without a doubt, blockchain is the way of the future. Despite a surge in interest in blockchain technology over the last few years, we are still in the very early phases of this field. Even if you are unfamiliar with blockchain technology now, in five or ten years, you will almost certainly be deemed an "early adopter" of the most disruptive technology since the Internet's inception.

## 7.4 Risk and Money Management

Money management is almost certainly the most critical idea in investing. If you lack a professional way to calculating the lot size, regardless of your trading technique, your account will be a non-starter. I am hoping that we can figure out how to calculate your risks together. Therefore, carefully examine the primary money management guidelines that I define for the cryptocurrency market.

**10% of the risk in a single trade:** That is, if you make a single trade, you will bear no more than 10% of the risk. If you make five trades each day, divide 10% of your risk by. Avoid numerous transactions in an attempt to increase your earnings. Paying commission fees to the exchange will cost you a lot of money.

**30% of cash in the account should always be the bare minimum:** Never invest entirely in cryptocurrencies or fiat currency. Even if the currency's value decreases, you should retain some cryptocurrency assets. Accordingly, when the market grows, you should hold less Bitcoins and more Ether and altcoins. The greater an asset's capitalization, the less volatile it is. Thus, if you desire less volatility in the fall, keep a portion of your funds in Bitcoin. Although 10%-20% of your total funds should be kept in cash, you should not retain everything in cash. If you own Bitcoin, you can buy altcoins, as they are frequently exchanged for Bitcoin. Simultaneously, you should have at least 30% of the cash on hand, especially during periods of rapid market expansion. You may require funds for a new intriguing initial money offering (ICO), a new altcoin movement, or something else.

**The rationale for entry and exit should be identical:** When you enter a trade, you should have an exit strategy in mind. Any scenario should have an exit strategy. All of your plans should be laid out in detail on paper, and you should not abandon them.

**Diversifying markets and assets:** If you are going to trade, you should do so on at least two respected exchanges. Take no risks, even if the newly opened exchange entices you with low fees or a bounty.

**Make few trades and abstain from gambling**: Here, you must determine the frequency with which you access the terminal and monitor the quotes. I advocate monitoring cryptocurrency activity no more than once a day. Choose a time of day when you feel most comfortable carrying out this task. For instance, you arrive home from work, pour a glass of red wine (or a cup of tea), and sit down peacefully to check on the latest developments in the cryptocurrency market. You are not need to obsessively monitor the market every ten minutes. This type of neurotic behavior is detrimental to both your health and your bank account.

**Have your own perspective and do not succumb to peer pressure:** There is no one on the planet who can tell you with certainty how much Bitcoin will cost tomorrow or make other accurate predictions. As a result, if you hear highly publicized projections in favor of a particular coin, this individual is almost certainly prejudiced in some way.

I remind you one again that nothing is definite. I recommend that you maintain a healthy skepticism at all times. Nobody knows what the future holds. Keep this in mind and you will see right through the scam. If someone persuades you of something, consider why this man is so adamant in proving his position. You can listen to other people's opinions, but you cannot invest in being guided by them.

**Keep the stop orders in mind**: As previously said, stop orders make no sense in the cryptocurrency market because they may not work or may perform poorly. As a result, always keep your stop (exit point) in mind or record it in a notepad. For instance, I purchased Ether for $250 with the intention of liquidating the position at $200.

I am sure you have realized by now that the cryptocurrency market is quite dangerous after reading this book. However, you will not be able to earn such gains anywhere else. Nowhere else in the world is it possible to double or triple an amount in a single day.

Finally, I want to emphasize that nothing is certain in the cryptocurrency market. If someone makes a guarantee to you, that person is a liar. Prepare for this, as similar scenarios occur frequently in this market. The most cunning and astute individuals (creators of initial coin offerings, experienced traders, and so on) compete in the cryptocurrency market, each pursuing their own objectives.

## 7.5 Investment Strategies

Would you rather make profits off your cryptocurrencies simply by purchasing Bitcoins or embrace more complex ideas? In the previous chapters of this book, I provided you with scenarios about how some of my students and friends accomplished their crypto goals. Surely, they all followed some of the most suitable investment strategies. It is vital to look at your chances of success while opting for a certain strategy.

Before going right to the strategies, you can employ in your cryptocurrency trading, let us have a look at the two major types of trading you can do in the current market.

### Margin Trading

Margin trading is straightforward. You trade borrowed money. When you buy on margin, you pay a portion of the stock price (referred to as the margin) and borrow the remainder from other market participants who are willing to lend you money. Your margin account balance is used just to represent this borrowed money and, if necessary, to cover loan expenses. In other words, margin trading enables you to trade with money that you do not possess. Leverage refers to the borrowed capital used in trade.

Assume that you have $10,000. It is, in a sense, your margin. Assume you choose to trade with a leverage of 1:4. This allows for a $40,000 transaction.

Your profit margin is 25%. You buy for $40,000, and if the purchased currency increases in value, your profit increases fourfold.

However, if the purchased currency decreases in value, your losses increase fourfold as well. Thus, if you buy $10,000 in cryptocurrencies, you risk losing all of your money only if the value of your asset (for example, Bitcoin) falls to zero.

However, if you invest $40,000 in cryptocurrencies using leverage on a margin account, you will lose all of your personal funds ($10,000) if the asset falls by 25%.

Consider another scenario: you maintain a margin position in Ether during a flash drop. In this situation, the exchange will close your position due to the fact that Ether had fallen more than 25% at the time. As soon as your loss reaches $10,000, the stock exchange will close your position at $40,000 in value. That is, $10,000 serves as collateral for your trade.

Margin or leverage is an excellent instrument for enhancing your profit in any other market. Almost every seasoned trader takes advantage of leverage. However, as previously said, the bitcoin market is extremely volatile, so leverage can literally destroy you. Why does this occur? Consider the stock market.

What could possibly cause Apple's stock to fall by, say, 20%? Nothing of the sort could happen, in my opinion. As a result, it is generally safe to trade Apple stock using leverage, as the stock cannot fall by more than 10% in a single day. Simultaneously, you can always take a position in the stock market, as trade is strictly controlled, and you can keep track of all happenings.

In contrast, the cryptocurrency market is open 24 hours a day, seven days a week.

Even the most illogical and nonsensical outcome is possible here because the price can increase or decrease by any proportion. As a result, if you are going to trade on margin in the bitcoin market, you would be wise to utilize a leverage ratio of 1:2. Leveraged trading is akin to Russian roulette. If you trade with a leverage of 1:4, your position is almost certain to be destroyed.

Always exercise caution: if you come across an exchange with a questionable interface or are offered 1:20 leverage, the exchange will likely look for marginal traders. It is on the lookout for greedy, crafty, and, as practice demonstrates, foolish traders looking to double their earnings instantly. As a result, let me reiterate that you should be verified on the leading exchanges if you choose to trade professionally. You should open at least two accounts for each of them.

You should have two margin accounts: one for your money and one for margin. To begin trading with leverage, you should move funds from your primary account to a margin account, from which you can trade.

Additionally, you should be familiar with the following aspects of margin trading. Do you believe you will be compensated for trading in money for nothing more than a "thank you?" Not. You will only be provided interest-bearing money. If you use 1:4 leverage and wish to trade $40,000 rather than $10,000, you will pay a higher interest rate. It can reach 1% to 2% per day. Interest accrues to a total of $30,000 in the matter at hand. I would want to remind you that you only have $10,000.

Finally, here are some beginner tips.

When you trade the market, you acquire assets whose value has plummeted precipitously. This is my principal strategy at the moment: to buy assets that are cheap or whose values have plummeted.

To close a position, place an order only if you have earned a profit of at least 50%. Waiting for higher profits is extremely dangerous, so close your position immediately after earning your 50%. Additionally, I do not advocate earning less than 10% profit. To my mind, 20% is the bare minimum you should aim for. However, if you engage in intraday trading, you may put sell orders at 30%+.

Bear in mind that the exchange charges a commission. The fewer trades you make, the greater the costs. And when your revenue increases, your commission rates decrease.

## Day Trading and Long Term Position Trading

Let us concentrate on your job schedule at the Bitcoin exchange.

Before you begin trading, you must make a critical decision on how much time you are willing to devote to trading. Of course, the optimal solution is to spend 5-6 hours a day at the computer, continually closing positions and monitoring the situation. However, due to a shortage of time, the majority of people now choose another choice. They trade goods once a week. On a given day, such traders review the week's news and any charts and then determine which positions to open or close.

Many individuals choose this route. Therefore, here are some pointers:

- Choose one day of the week that you will devote exclusively to trading.

- On this day, examine your portfolio to determine which currencies have increased in value and which have decreased in value.

Keep an eye on the news. Make judgments based on current events and the mix of your portfolio. If the value of an asset has not increased or has even decreased, close the position. If you see anything that appears to be promising or is on price, buy it. You should do these transactions on each day of the week that you have designated for trading. By the way, I propose Blockfolio as a more convenient way to track your positions.

To summarize, I recommend one of the two approaches to trading: daily monitoring with limited sell orders or weekly monitoring.

Simultaneously, certain cryptocurrency exchanges, such as Bitfinex, provide OTC trading. The abbreviation OTC stands for Over the Counter, which refers to a transaction that occurs over the counter. This is a decentralized market that lacks a central physical location and in which market participants trade assets via the dealers' network.

For instance, if you lack time to monitor the market and are completely focused on trading via order placement, you can utilize the services of this market. Your cooperation will be conducted over the phone or by e-mail. Thus, you inform a trader that you wish to buy 250 bitcoins. After perusing the market, the dealer determines how much you should pay for this amount of bitcoins. For this service, the dealer will charge a fee.

Below are some of the crypto investment strategies:

## Buy Bitcoin

As a result of this method, all you need to do is to purchase Bitcoin. This technique is optimal in every way. It is straightforward to apply, and you will not be required to delve into the complexities of economic or technical principles. As a result, this method may yield the greatest profit.

## Follow The Money

Here, I recommend that you purchase a set number of different coins from the top ten greatest cryptocurrencies available today.

In other words, you will acquire several market leaders. The coins, whose value would surge, will compensate for the losses incurred due to the failure of the other coins. Additionally, this technique entails enormous risks.

Nothing can shield you from the reality that coins that have appeared to be stable in the past year may experience a significant decline in value next year. However, you should keep in mind that there are currently no fundamental reasons for Bitcoin to fail, which could be triggered, for example, by its incapacity to survive competition from other currencies. This is a distinct possibility, if only because Bitcoin is one of the most technically vulnerable coins.

## Trading

While many people associate trading with analysis, patterns, and technical modeling, the trader's task is a subjective judgment of market conditions.

Apart from having a glass of whiskey (grin), the first thing a competent trader should do is forecast which cryptocurrencies will grow in the market. Following that, traders must forecast the optimal entry point into the market.

What comes next?

They should continue forecasting when coin prices would begin to decrease. However, the most critical aspect of trading is having enormous expertise and even a small bit of luck. Additionally, a trader must consistently repeat all of the preceding procedures.

This is an issue since rarely everything works out as planned, yet risks must constantly be assumed.

That is why, in my opinion, trading suits those with an engineering mindset, ample time, and, most importantly, a strong spirit.

Mining

This approach requires primarily computer equipment to execute.

**What comes next?** You insert it into a socket and wait for the money to flow into your pocket.

**What do you use the money for?**

As previously stated, miners are compensated for providing computational capacity to the network. In addition, the network compensates miners with coins in exchange for their equipment and labor.

## ICOs (Initial Coin Offerings)

The bitcoin market now provides additional options for active investors. This strategy is ideal if you have a lot of spare time (and money), sufficient experience, and a desire to earn large and quick gains. However, while this strategy is extremely profitable, it is also extremely hazardous, especially for novices.

The fundamental tenet of ICO strategy, which I also refer to as startups, is as follows.

The Bitcoin economy has created an incredibly simple method for individuals with unique and exciting ideas to support their endeavors. They no longer need to pound the pavement, begging and persuading large firms to invest in their idea. Instead, these innovators and developers can now post a proposal on their website. Then, if you are interested in their concept, you can publish your wallet's address to receive tokens if the concept proves successful.

The consequence is that you will have to invest money now to reap a profit later.

Historically, the regulations of ICOs were pretty straightforward.

I pay you one dollar, and you give me two tokens. Now, some initial coin offerings (ICOs) go to ludicrous lengths. In general, after investing in an ICO, you may discover that you can exchange your tokens only on Friday at midnight during the full moon and only if you are a mermaid with a blue tail. Perhaps my story is a bit exaggerated, but it exemplifies the obscurity of the regulations that govern most companies (ICOs).

If it was not difficult to locate a grain of truth amid the diversity of ICOs half a year ago (when just a handful debuted in a week and could be readily evaluated), now new ICOs occur virtually every hour, and you do not have time to evaluate them all.

### What would I advise a newcomer enticed to try his luck with initial coin offerings?

First, you must have a firm grasp of the business area in which you intend to invest. If you are knowledgeable about it, you can assess it and determine if it has a chance of success.

Additionally, I suggest you to heed what experienced investors and professionals have to say and disregard what is mentioned on the ICO's website.

I would even argue that you should avoid investing in any initial coin offering that is not referenced in at least three professional analytical studies written by acknowledged professionals.

Penny Stocks

If you are familiar with the exchange trade, you should be familiar with the concept of penny stocks. To put it bluntly, these are shares in the company that nobody needs.

However, these shares have one advantage: they are so inexpensive that nothing can prevent them from doubling in value.

Such a miraculous surge can occur as a result of excellent news, a little market manipulation, or for any other reason. Therefore, how can you make use of this strategy?

You purchase the most unusual and obscure coins and then wait to watch how the scenario develops. Throughout the year, the value of some of your coins may increase. If this occurs, you should sell this currency immediately. If you purchased fifty coins, a price increase of even one super-cheap coin would compensate for the loss of your entire investment portfolio. This strategy precludes you from delving deeply into the fundamentals of the Bitcoin business.

All you have to do is purchase "trash" and sell it on time. However, this strategy is not within my purview because it resembles a casino. You do not require any talents or education, only good fortune. You have no control over what happens or how risks are managed because everything is contingent on good fortune.

**Follow My Steps**

This strategy is ideal if you lack knowledge in the bitcoin industry but have money to dabble with. However, you must be willing to accept risks and entrust your money to strangers. Because the bitcoin industry is unregulated, nobody can ensure that a corporation or someone who claimed to earn money for you would not take your money and flee to some sunny destination.

Numerous businesses on the market offer profit in exchange for trust. For example, some companies provide mining contracts to those interested in mining without investing in the necessary equipment and space. This is referred to as cloud mining.

**A different form of business is cryptocurrency funds.**

These companies have no idea how to mine but are adept at estimating good coins.

The third category is the initial coin offering mutual funds. These people spend their time scouring the market for startups in which they will subsequently invest your money. Finally, there is trading. You cede ownership of your money to someone else, who will trade on your behalf.

After discussing these investment techniques, please understand that I do not consider these strategies perfect. Therefore, allow me to share two perfect investment strategies with you.

**There are, in my opinion, two ideal strategies.**

The first is based on your honest belief in the future of Bitcoin.

If this describes you, you should take on a few methods that interest you, mix them up, and begin profiting in this manner: by diversifying your possibilities of profiting as well as your risks.

If you believe in the future of the bitcoin company, you should focus on the second ideal investment strategy:

**Profit from others who do.**

Some people will require mining equipment and premises, some will require dollars, and still, others will require information, and you can earn money by meeting their demands.

# 7.6 Trader Mindset

You will undoubtedly agree that the psychological mindset required to excel in any undertaking is critical. Some people are born with the appropriate mindset, while others must work to develop it.

In either case, I want to emphasize a few critical principles that can help you profit from the cryptocurrency market or, at the very least, prevent significant losses.

**Avoid being greedy:** Do not wait for the price to increase more to profit even more. Your avarice may cost you not only profits but also a loss.

**Maintain patience:** If you buy a currency at a specific price and do not notice significant upward or downward movement, do not panic and sell it quickly. I have witnessed numerous instances of a cryptocurrency's nearly constant price suddenly doubling in a week. You may be wondering how to avoid a loss during a market correction. My response is this: do not convert all of your cryptocurrency to fiat currency! Numerous people make this error and eventually regret it. You would be wise to check theme forums and user reviews of this coin before selling everything.

**Always keep in mind the market's depth:** When there are a large number of sellers and a small number of buyers, you can acquire some assets at an ostensibly attractive price but fail to sell everything you have acquired.

Keep an eye on the market capitalization and trading volume of a cryptocurrency.

**You should follow these steps:**

This is to ascertain whether spikes will be present. Thus, after analyzing cryptocurrency price fluctuations and identifying specific patterns, you can develop your strategy and trading plan. Then, you can begin refining it under real-world situations by beginning with tiny quantities that practically all transactions allow. Finally, if your method proves effective, you can increase your investments gradually.

Finally, I summarize my concise and efficient advice once more. I hope they are beneficial in assisting you in becoming a successful cryptocurrency investor.

Contrary to popular belief, do not alter your plan at every opportunity. Profit from your efforts. Do not lose sight of your primary objectives. Make no rash decisions. Automate as many processes as feasible.

# Conclusion

At the outset of this book, I stated that many individuals do not take cryptocurrency seriously due to the market's numerous fallacies. Let us now summarize and eventually debunk these falsehoods.

To begin, many people believe that the most essential and attractive aspect of the cryptocurrency market is the opportunity for enormous profits, and they enter the market solely for this reason. On the other hand, profit is a completely secondary goal that may be achieved in any business, in my opinion. The question is, how willing are you to take risks? As a result, the most critical aspect of cryptocurrency is risk.

Simultaneously, it is asserted that the cryptocurrency market's profit-to-risk ratio is highly distorted. According to some, if you take a modest risk in another market and get a modest profit, you can earn hundreds of times more in this market by taking the same amount of risk. That is not the case. Profits to risks are always nearly equal. If it were indeed possible to earn a significant profit while taking minimal risks, Swiss banks would be depleted of cash, as everyone would have already invested in this business.

Many others claim that it is too late to enter the cryptocurrency market because it has only gained popularity and has generated and distributed all profits. I concur with the notion that it would be difficult for newbies because of the cryptocurrency frenzy, but is this reason to believe it is too late to enter the market and obtain your profits? If you continue to study, strive, and attempt, you will also begin to earn decent money. Perseverance always pays off. While it may need additional time and resources, a slogger will undoubtedly be rewarded with success.

Apart from the belief that it is too late to enter the market, some argue that this market is only accessible to programmers and professional traders. This is a fabrication. You can also earn a lot of money in the cryptocurrency market if you are a doctor, a teacher, or a middle-ranking manager. Regardless of one's current skill level, one can learn the necessary information and gain the necessary skills. For example, nobody is born an artist, but everyone may learn to draw by learning various drawing techniques.

I am not sure what conclusions you came to following your reading of my book. However, I hope that you now recognize cryptocurrency as a present-day reality rather than a distant possibility.

The sooner you grasp this, the further you may pull yourself away from the locomotive's skeptics. As a result, I strongly advise you to embrace cryptocurrency.

If you read this book from the start to the very end, I also feel that I have assisted you in not just debunking cryptocurrency myths and fundamentals but also in laying the groundwork for a prosperous long-term business in this space. Although a cornerstone has been set, this is only the beginning. Everything is now dependent on you. Consider knowledge in the sense that the only way to learn and receive something is through trial and error. Take your first steps into the cryptocurrency market by employing the safest tactics possible.

Now I would like to address individuals who believe that no particular effort is required in this business. You may believe that simply pressing the "start" button will result in money falling from the sky.

However, if you have already envisaged yourself relaxing by the seashore, expecting that the cryptocurrency business will enable you to travel constantly without having to work, you are quite mistaken. As with any other business, this one demands you to get off the couch and put your strength, wits, and money to work to build a prosperous future.

The primary requirement is that you believe in yourself and cryptocurrency.

After all, individuals who believed in Bitcoin a few years ago now own enormous wealth and influence. As a result, I believe in the cryptocurrency economy's dawn!

**Finally, a few words of advice.**

To begin, you should not take cryptocurrency very seriously. The cryptocurrency market is extremely volatile, and unless you develop a healthy fear of risk and loss, you will drive yourself insane. It is preferable to approach this business with an open mind from the start. I believe that survival in the cryptocurrency market is impossible without a sense of humor and perhaps a few curse words. At the same time, this is not a casino or a lottery. You need a clear strategy and a strong sense of purpose to succeed in the cryptocurrency market.

Second, as we covered at the beginning of the book, you must use caution and skepticism when working in this market.

Thus, my dear reader, I sincerely hope that you will stop simply following cryptocurrency news and begin earning money in this market after reading this book.

Sort out the nuances of this subject for good and be capable of identifying cryptocurrency scammers. Then, choose the finest strategy for profiting in the cryptocurrency market for you. Invest your money wisely, and you can earn a handsome profit. Finally, discover a source of semi-passive income and consider quitting your work if you are sick and bored of it.

Develop hundreds of beneficial relationships with investors and cryptocurrency entrepreneurs.

**Realize your goals.**

www.ingramcontent.com/pod-product-compliance
Lightning Source LLC
Chambersburg PA
CBHW071711210326
41597CB00017B/2431